Going Back to Work

A SURVIVAL GUIDE FOR COMEBACK MOMS

Mary W. Quigley and
Loretta E. Kaufman

ST. MARTIN'S GRIFFIN
NEW YORK

www.stmartins.com

Library of Congress Cataloging-in-Publication Data

Quigley, Mary W., 1949–
    Going back to work : a survival guide for comeback moms / by Mary W.
Quigley and Loretta E. Kaufman.
        p.   cm.
    ISBN 0-312-31321-7
    EAN 978-0312-31321-0
    1. Working mothers.   2. Women—employment.   I. Kaufman, Loretta,
1944–   II. Title.
HQ759.48.Q54 2004
306.874'3—dc22   2003026316

10   9   8   7   6   5   4   3

To our children

Colleen, Sean, and Brendan and Joan
Jim and Julia, Liz and David

For the enthusiastic support and encouragement
Of their own comeback moms

Contents

Going Back to Work

Introduction

ON MOTHER'S DAY 2000, we set off on a tour to promote our first book about stay-at-home moms. As we headed cross-country, we had our antennae up for static signaling the subject for our next book. From a shopping mall in Houston to a bookstore in Minneapolis, from a café in Pasadena to a library meeting room on Long Island, woman after woman told us that while she treasured the years at home, she definitely planned to go back to work at some point. The message was the same whether it was from new moms in their thirties or older moms in their late forties with teens (and sometimes toddlers too). They all planned on "going back." Some moms who had stayed home from day one planned to go back when their youngest went off to kindergarten; others had worked through the first baby or two and quit when their children got older and their lives more complicated. Often we spent an hour or more after a book talk chatting and fielding questions about overcoming the obstacles to going back.

At one point, we quipped, "Remember, we're journalists not therapists!"

And so the idea for this book grew and developed. To the dozens upon dozens of women we spoke to personally around the country, we added hundreds upon hundreds more from an online survey at our Web site. Some mothers had returned to work, others were looking ahead. All told, we heard from more than one thousand women while researching and reporting this book. The number-one work issue? Flexibility. The women stated loud and clear that flexibility means more than an occasional afternoon off for a doctor's appointment or school recital. Rather, it means flexible hours in the form of telecommuting, a compressed workweek, job sharing, variable start/end times, and part-time work.

If I Can't See You, You're Not Working

Just as adamant as their cry for flexibility was the lament that, with some exceptions, American business still does not embrace the concept. As one young South Carolina mother said, "I think companies hire consultants who tell them that to attract educated workers they need to use buzzwords like 'family-friendly' and 'flexibility.' But they really don't know how to implement those practices." While many companies have policies on the books, the reality is that it all comes down to the office culture and the direct supervisor. Too many bosses still subscribe to the if-I-can't-see-you-you're-not-working theory of management, despite functioning in a high-tech world.

Flexibility was followed closely by decent pay, benefits, emotional satisfaction, and (maybe) respect. Can it happen? It already has. Thousands of women are not waiting for a declaration of social change. Many women we spoke to, regardless of age, wanted to switch careers or work part-time or start their own business or spin a variation on the traditional notion of work. And career is just one part of the puzzle. Children, husbands, aging parents, child care, younger (and older) coworkers, technology, work ethics, personal interests, and more were all pieces that had to fit together.

The women in this book are breaking new ground, cutting a path through obstacles, and fashioning work that works for them and their families. "The returning mom is a pioneer and she's charting new terrain as she makes her way through the work world," says Kathleen Christensen, program director for the Alfred P. Sloan Foundation's Workplace, Workforce and Working Families project, a major funder of research on work and family. The work-family experts tell us that institutional change is necessary to truly transform the American workplace so that motherhood and career are not mutually exclusive. That has not happened. Instead, these new ways of working are being fashioned by individuals rather than institutions. The women in this book are the pioneers, leading the way for other moms.

Forging a New Path

We found hundreds of women in cities, suburbs, and rural communities who were quietly and creatively fashioning work that works, from Alaska where a mom toted her infant along to her teacher certification classes, to Atlanta where a former computer saleswoman started a home-based public relations business with her husband, to Maine where a career counselor has combined two part-time jobs, to New York where a mother of three boys became an Episcopal priest, to California where a longtime

3

at-home mom worked her way up to an assistant director of development at a major law school in fewer than five years. We talked to women who after years at home started second careers as a trauma counselor for 9/11 families, a molecular biologist, a youth program director, an aquarium guide, college professors, consultants, nurses, teachers, and more. Dr. Christensen says that young women today need role models for combining family and work. You'll find them in this book!

A Family-Friendly Workplace?

Flexibility does not mean a gym at work or a concierge or a cafeteria. Those are all perks that help us work better, not promote family life. "I feel that what we often call family-friendly is often work-friendly in the sense that it frees the workers from family responsibilities so they can concentrate more on their jobs," says Dr. Phyllis Moen, who holds the McKnight Presidential Chair in sociology at the University of Minnesota.

Our survey results also found that the desire for flexibility stems from the worry about time: not having enough of it. More than 75 percent of our survey women noted that the biggest problem of going back to work was lack of time for their children, their husbands, and themselves. Our survey results echoed other research. The Sloan 500 Family study found that nearly two-thirds of moms who currently work full-time would rather be working part-time. About 40 percent of those mothers find that job and family life come into conflict almost all the time.[1] Dr. Moen's Ecology of Careers study of more than twenty-two hundred people found similar results. "Study after study shows that people want more free time. Nearly half of all the couples report preferences for ideal work hours lower than their actual hours worked. Most respondents work the hours they do simply because their jobs require it, not because of personal motivation or household level demand," notes Dr. Moen, in her book *It's About Time*.[2] A 2003 *Redbook* survey found that 61 percent of moms who work full-time say they'd like part-time or flex hours, but one out of four is afraid to ask because she fears jeopardizing her job.[3]

Who Is the Ideal Worker?

Since the 1990s, more and more academics have been drawn to the study of what they view as a pressing societal issue. Anthropologists, sociologists, psychologists, labor economists, and others have conducted studies, written theses, and taught courses in the academic field called "work-family." The Sloan Foundation sponsors research projects on Workplace, Workforce and Working Families at six universities, all in an effort to discover how to better manage work and family. What has all the research found? The basic problem is that, even in the twenty-first century, business is still designed for what American University law professor Joan Williams calls the "ideal worker": a man who works continuously for forty years and whose wife takes care of the family so he can work long hours. That was June and Ward Cleaver, who today exist only in reruns. Now the stay-at-home mom has typically clocked a decade or more of work BC (before children) and goes back to resume her career or start a new one as the children enter school. Other moms move in and out of the labor force to start their own businesses, care for an ailing parent, provide hands-on supervision for older children, and myriad other life situations. But business seemingly wears blinders when it comes to stops and starts on career paths and sees only the organization man. Dr. Moen maintains that there is a "mismatch between real lives and outdated work and career-path roles." The way work is structured, whether the assembly line or the boardroom, has changed very little in the last half century, despite the changes in family life with dual-career couples.

The careers paths of stay-at-home moms are deeply affected by this fundamental problem of "structural mismatch" between workplace and the workers, says Dr. Christensen. "The conventional wisdom is that the person who doesn't make a career mark by her early thirties has minimized her options for success. An ideal career path is seen as getting on in the twenties, success in the thirties, and plateauing in the forties. That career model works for men but is a problem for women who want to take time off or work less when they have families."

Little recognition is given to the fact that men's work lives are changing too. Over the last decade it has become politically correct for men to leave work early to coach a soccer team or attend a school recital. Younger men especially want to play a bigger role in their children's lives and, although we don't expect a demographic explosion of Mr. Moms, more fathers are assuming responsibility on the home front so their wives can return to work. In fact, many of the survey women noted that they were able to resume demanding careers because their husbands modified their own work schedules. Flexibility is not just a women's issue.

Baby Boomer and Gen-X Moms

Changes are slowly occurring. Over the next few years business will find itself sandwiched between both Gen-X and baby boomer moms. The boomer moms who fought for equal opportunity now are reluctant to leave the office. Whether it's the idea that work keeps you young or the reality of bear market retirement funds, many of these women—and men—are not cashing out at age sixty-five. "Baby boomers are the leading wedge for getting flex work more accepted. Many older workers either need to or want to continue to work beyond retirement, but not necessarily full-time, full-year work," says Dr. Christensen, whose program at the Alfred P. Sloan Foundation has recently launched an initiative working with business, labor, government, and advocacy groups to create more flexible options, including career paths with multiple points of entry, exit, and reentry.

So it seems that the boomers who managed to influence every decade over the last forty years will continue right through the beginning of the twenty-first century, going out with a bang not a whimper. *Wall Street Journal* work and family columnist Sue Shellenbarger agrees. "Corporate America will want to keep some older workers who won't say, 'How high should I jump?' and who will insist on more part-time schedules and more autonomy. That will force the redesign of work as more managers address work load and restructure some jobs."

The Gen-X moms carry a sense of entitlement. From their earliest days these young women were told they could be whatever they wanted, and no one added, "Oh, by the way, if you stop working for children your career will derail." Gen-X moms have made it clear they want more control over their lives and want to work on their terms. They expect to combine stay-at-home motherhood with contemporary work. Unlike their older sisters, they are not shy about asking for flexible schedules and, what's more, expect an affirmative answer. "I don't have any hard data, but I have talked to about a million women about this," Professor Williams said with a laugh one winter's day on a New York City visit. "I have noticed a real generational shift. Women over fifty were just so grateful to be allowed into the workforce that it never occurred to us for one millisecond to demand changes. But women in their twenties and thirties feel entitled to be in the workplace and also feel entitled to live up to traditional ideas of motherhood. They think it is completely inappropriate for employers to make demands that are incompatible with motherhood."

There is a generation gap, agrees Kirsten Ross, founder of Womans-Work.com, which helps women find alternative job arrangements. "Older women say, 'We fought so hard to get these opportunities. Why are you ruining it all by not playing by the rules?' Younger women say, 'That was *your* fight. We want careers with flexibility.'"

A possible labor shortage is also expected to aid the push toward a more flexible workplace. The Bureau of Labor Statistics predicts that the number of available jobs will increase by 15 percent, or twenty-two million jobs, by 2010. But the labor force is projected to increase by only seventeen million people by 2010.[4] Theoretically at least, businesses will be forced to offer more flexibility to retain skilled workers.

Going Back Doesn't Mean Forty Hours a Week

We know from our first book that women left their careers to stay home full-time primarily because they wanted to raise their children themselves and found this impossible to do while running like a hamster around a cage called work. From our research for this book, we know that when those stay-at-home moms get ready to return they don't want to jump right back on the same treadmill. Going back is not a matter of waving good-bye at the kindergarten door and plunging into a forty-hour workweek. Many mothers realize that hands-on parenting is needed in the tween and teen years, maybe not 24/7, but not the latchkey model, either. Other factors come into play too. While money, obviously, is also a key consideration, emotional and intellectual rewards are right up there at the top of the list. "I am not going back to work and leaving my children unless I can find a job that is emotionally fulfilling," says one Brooklyn mom.

The women in this book approach work the second time around with renewed enthusiasm and energy. Yes, they may have some catching up to do but, to their surprise and delight, ambition often kicks in and they are achieving new goals, and then some. Their enlightened employers often find they receive an unexpected bonus with a highly motivated worker who doesn't take lunch or chitchat around the coffee machine. "If you give them an inch they will give back a mile. It's time to lose the stereotype that anyone working less than full-time is not serious or dedicated to her career," says Ellen Galinsky, president and cofounder of the Families and Work Institute.

So join us as we hear the tales of their travels and how they survived the inevitable bumps and detours along the career path. We offer the nuts and bolts of how to get back into the game. More important, we take a holistic approach and help fit together all the pieces of the career puzzle—self, family, and work—so they can complement and enhance each other.

One
Making the Decision

WHEN YOU PUSHED the business suits to the back of the closet you always imagined that someday you'd take them out, see if they still fit, and then head back to work. But in those intervening years of playgroups and PTA meetings, that crystal ball became clouded by many unanswered questions.

While at home, you may have rethought your priorities, now very different from BC (before children). The goals that propelled you down one career path in your twenties no longer ignite you in your thirties or forties. Needs are different. Interests have changed. Bankers want to be more creative; nurses don't want to work in medicine; teachers don't want to go back to the classroom. Mothers and More, a national organization for stay-at-home moms, found in a survey that about 71 percent of its members plan to return to work. Yet the survey also found that more than one-third do not plan to return to the same occupation and another third are undecided about their career path.[1] So how do you decide? As many of us say with a nervous laugh, "I don't know what I want to be when I grow up."

Going back is further complicated by uncertainty. Should you go back fairly quickly, after three years or less at home when—maybe—someone at your old office still remembers your name? What about waiting until the "baby" is in first grade? Wait until middle school? But then the kids need you during those turbulent tween years. Maybe you should wait until the nest is almost empty.

Then there are those practical problems. How do you explain that big black hole in your résumé? Former business contacts have been replaced by women from "mommy and me" classes. Computer skills? Sure, you surf the Web for airline fares, but what about putting data on a spreadsheet, preparing a PowerPoint presentation, or putting up a Web site, all standard operating procedures in most offices these days. Rapidly changing industries? Companies have closed, regrouped, and changed names in the time you've been gone. Perhaps a stumbling block is a lack of self-confidence. We've all heard women complain that "my mind turned to mush" at home. Can you go out there and slay dragons with the guys? Can you still competently handle crabby coworkers, crying kindergartners, critically ill patients, cranky customers?

"I Am Going Back to Work"

From speaking to hundreds of women, we learned that the number-one fear among stay-at-home moms is getting caught up in a maelstrom of work and not having enough time for husband and family, to say nothing of themselves. What's the point of going back to the same out-of-control treadmill that you jumped off a few years ago? How can the thirty- to fortysomething woman saddled with her own self-doubt and faced with multiple challenges at home take this giant step? How do you turn wishful thinking into the powerful statement, "I am going back to work and this is how I am going about it"?

We are going to help you. Step one, buy a notebook and get into the habit of writing in it. Forget the black speckled school notebook; buy something classy. Think of it as an agenda with an agenda (yours!) where you will note your thoughts, hopes, and goals. Writing things down is nothing new to moms. Lists are our lifelines: calories, budgeting, moving, getting ready for a vacation, back-to-school shopping. This is your career baby book, not unlike the book in which you carefully recorded your toddler's first steps.

Start by keeping an ongoing list of your accomplishments as a stay-at-home mom. From organizing a family reunion with relatives from six states to supervising a kitchen remodeling, women have developed skills at home that will serve them well in the workplace. Write it all down. You'll never remember everything when you're trying to compose your résumé. Writing it down will also help clarify your thinking as you dissect your decision to return and try to answer questions about timing and money.

Dissecting the Decision

"My epiphany moment was one of those mornings when the kids were both under two. I was in pajamas and my husband was ready

to do his court thing. He took out a big bottle of orange juice, and it dropped and shattered. I was in the middle of the sea of juice and glass when he ran off to court . . . I cannot live the rest of my life like this."

"I was going crazy staying at home. I felt like I was losing brain mass every day I was at home."

"Even though financially it is a wash for me to work after child care, taxes, tithe, clothing, etc., I view it as a social outlet and as an alternative to antidepressants."

"I am going back to work for security. I don't want to be left standing in the cold, especially since I gave up further schooling to put my husband through dental school."

"We needed the money . . . my husband was fired."

"It was time."

"I want to return to the workforce for personal growth."

The reasons for going back vary from personal fulfillment to personal finance with dozens of permutations in between. We know without a doubt that one day when everything goes wrong at work and you arrive home tired and stressed, you'll ask yourself, "Why did I ever go back?" It's important to carefully consider your reasons.

One thing you need before you reenter is a clear sense, a realistic sense, of your goals. "What do you hope to get out of going back to work?" asks Shelley MacDermid, director of the Purdue University Center for Families. "Leaving home to go to work for a few hours is not going to solve everything in your life. You must be clear on what your goals are and your chances for achieving them."

Before delving into all the good reasons to go back to work, let's remember what going back to work *won't* do for you. It's just like that myth that if you diet down to a size ten then your life will be perfect. As any size ten will tell you, that simply isn't true. Going back to work will not solve all your problems. If you're unhappy with yourself, your children, or your husband, don't expect those troubles simply to go away when you walk out the door nicely dressed in the morning.

Even with the best-laid plans, life does not always flow smoothly. The day your child comes down with strep throat will be, guaranteed, the same day your annual report or presentation is due. You will once again pull all-nighters. You will be so stressed out that you will consider curling up with a pint of ice cream. (Remember: *Desserts* is *stressed* backward!)

Going back may not be forever. You may get back to work and everything is progressing smoothly, and suddenly there are some bumps in the road. Maybe the child-care arrangements fall apart, or your job-share partner gets pregnant and leaves. There can be a dozen different reasons. After three years back at ABC television as an advertising salesperson, Diane Gartner of Atlantic Beach, New York, gave up the plum job when faced with a triple challenge: three children enrolled in three different schools, traveling on three different buses. "I was a little overwhelmed with all their activities," Diane says. "Things were getting a little hectic. The kids were in a good, regimented schedule, and now, all of a sudden, everything changed. I felt I needed to come home and get reorganized again."

That doesn't mean that Diane won't return to work at some

point when her children are older. By going back the first time she proved that she can play the game with the big boys and girls again. But Diane and other women realize that the so-called work-family balance requires recalibrating the scales on occasion. Diane explains, "The greatest thing working gave me was balance. It gave me an opportunity to step out of the world of being mommy to Rachel, Nicole, and Evan and becoming Diane again for a little bit, which you can start to lose at home. Then, after working for three years, I was becoming too much Diane and not enough mommy."

Going back is fraught with decisions: when, where, and how? You stare at the blank page in your agenda. There are so many questions that you are unsure where to begin. We have discovered if you focus on three major questions, the answers will come a little easier.

A Job or a Career?

The first basic question to consider: a job or a career? What's the difference? In the most simple terms, it's a difference of time and emotional commitment. A job is a closed-end work situation where you can easily leave at quitting time and don't answer e-mail or pages after hours. You are looking for the satisfaction of a job well done, adult camaraderie, and a paycheck . . . period. When Debbie Mahoney of Dix Hills, New York, went back to work, she was looking for a job. Her four boys, aged thirteen, eleven, ten, and five, were in school full-time and her husband worked long hours. We chatted over lunch on the patio of the hospital where she now works as a medical staff administrator, and Debbie recalled with exasperation, "I just wanted a job where I could put on a suit and makeup a few days a week and make some new friends."

Because Debbie had not worked since the birth of her oldest son, reentering the workforce even on a part-time basis was a major psychological step, so she returned to the same hospital she had left at age twenty-five. Debbie also knew she could not jump into a full-time career with four children needing marathon car pooling from three P.M. to nine P.M, a household to manage, and a husband often halfway around the world. So she started slowly, working fifteen hours a week in a clerical support position. The first step was difficult after so many years, but she was determined. "My life was extremely quiet from eight A.M. to three P.M., so much so that I knew I had to make my move," she says. "I actually had begun taking art classes before I returned to work to fill my days, and was very active in the elementary school for several years. Eventually it just wasn't enough."

Debbie's Reasons for Going Back
- to regain confidence
- to be challenged
- to feel a sense of accomplishment beyond wife and mother

For Debbie, it was simply a job. Other moms, especially those who have kept a hand in, opt to go back on a career track, with more opportunity and responsibility. Mona Behan, a former magazine writer and editor, stayed home for nine years with her two children in a suburban community about twenty-five miles south of San Francisco. Mona kept her skills fresh by freelancing, including writing numerous magazine articles, contributing lodging and restaurant reviews to guidebooks, and cowriting a nonfiction book, *Warrior Women*,[2] with a Berkeley archaeologist. She says with a chuckle, "The archaeologist was the brains and I was the brawn." As her children grew into teenagers she decided to go back to work.

Mona's Reasons for Going Back
- to find intellectual challenges in a congenial atmosphere
- to explore the world of new technology
- to prove to herself that "this old brain could learn new tricks"

A serendipitous meeting at an open-school night led Mona to an editing job at a parenting and medical advice Web site, Dr.Spock.com. She took on the challenge and learned how to edit and input copy for the Web. The payoff was a lot more than a good salary and health benefits. It was just the jump start she needed. "I have a renewed sense of confidence in my work ability," says Mona. "I also learned I am not a creaky dinosaur."

Other women, often those who left well-paying, challenging careers, want to prove that they can play the game again. Until the birth of her second child, Diane, the ABC-TV ad sales rep, worked for eight years making presentations, doing market research, and closing deals. Then she quit and moved to suburbia. The opportunity to go back came when several ABC sales reps became pregnant and the company wanted to hire temporary replacements. Diane, who by that time had a third child, went back for a three-month stint. That became six months, and then ABC, impressed with her work, offered her a full-time position.

Diane didn't want to work long hours five days a week, so she arranged a job share. "What I got out of going back was the fact that I could do it again," Diane says. "You know, you stay home and you start to wonder about your ability to generate revenue and negotiate like I used to, which was a big part of my job. I learned that I could still do it and that I still enjoyed doing it. And it was a part of who I am. It made me feel very good about myself."

A job or career also depends on how much time and emotional commitment you want to invest. Other considerations will impact on your thinking as well. While many survey women noted that they returned to work for financial reasons, they also ranked an increased sense of self-esteem and achievement right up there along with money. Also, perhaps inspired by years of paging through magazine makeovers, many women decide that returning to work is a great time to reinvent themselves. Who couldn't use a little reinvention now and then? Remember the sense of opportunity you felt when you graduated from college? Imagine that feeling again, this time with the advantage of wisdom gained over the ensuing years. Mona's position at The Dr. Spock Company reinvigorated her. "When you come out of college you see the world of possibility," she says. "Then you get closed up in suburban family life and don't peek over the fence. But now even at the ripe old age of forty-seven I feel a sense of choice and possibility, and it's all very invigorating like the same feeling as a new college graduate." That feeling often comes from the realization that it's your turn to pursue your dreams, and that with two decades or more of paid work still ahead of you, there's time to follow your new ambitions.

CONSIDER THESE QUESTIONS ABOUT A CAREER:

- Is my work more than an income and an integral part of my identity?
- Am I willing to let my work take precedence at times over my family?
- Am I willing to be available by cell phone and e-mail day or night, come in early, stay late, and travel?
- Am I willing to be transferred and move?
- Am I willing to take a promotion with greater responsibility—and longer hours?

IF THOSE QUESTIONS SEND YOUR BLOOD PRESSURE SOARING, THEN MAYBE YOU WANT A JOB:

- I want to work clearly defined hours and leave my work worries at the office.
- I am working primarily for income and contact with adults.
- I accept the fact that my job may offer little potential for advancement.
- I am not willing to be transferred.
- I am not willing to go beyond my present level of time commitment.
- I understand that I might not be intellectually challenged by my work, and that's okay.

Now It's My Turn

Even women with a strong sense of self-esteem sometimes feel that their family's needs and wants have gotten priority over their own . . . for five years, ten years, or more. Now it's their turn to pursue a goal and give that priority. Mary started on her first book when the second of her three children entered his senior year in high school. After almost twenty years of raising children and teaching at NYU, there was finally some "free" time on the horizon. The amount of effort a book requires meant saying no sometimes to her children, but after all those years of putting their needs first, there should be no guilt. Well, okay, there was guilt, but she got used to it!

Sometimes "my turn" is long deferred, especially when it is a dream held since childhood. While it's hard to become a brain surgeon or rocket scientist at age thirty or forty, there are many careers that can be deferred and even enhanced by the ups and downs of raising children. That certainly is the case for Brenda Overfield, an Episcopal priest from Valley Stream, New York. Although Reverend Overfield, or Mother Brenda as she prefers, believes that she had a religious calling since age ten, she waited until her three sons were out of diapers and settled before embarking on the rigorous path to becoming a priest. One spring day, we met for lunch to talk about her deferred dream. That afternoon she was going to visit a ninety-year-old parishioner in the hospital, so she was wearing clerical garb. Even in blasé New York, heads turned at the sight of an attractive blonde wearing a white clerical collar and black shirt. Mother Brenda is used to the reaction and laughingly recalled an incident when she was a hospital chaplain. "The patient saw me with the collar and says, 'You're a woman!' Without missing a beat I said, 'Oh, my God! I am.'"

While growing up as an "air force brat" and moving around the country, "I had a sense of God in my life, of something deep inside of me calling me to serve the church," she says. Soon after graduating from the University of Missouri, she married her college sweetheart, a navy officer, and gave birth to three sons over a period of six years. Yet her dream of becoming an Episcopal priest was always on her mind. "I was raising the boys and committed to staying at home. I would have conversations with God but knew it was not the time yet." Then over a few months a string of coincidences occurred. "A girlfriend gave me a Bible for 'when you become a priest,' and I hadn't said anything to her about that. The same with an aunt who gave me a cross for 'when you're ordained.' These were all signs that the time was right." While living in Virginia, Brenda applied to a seminary program. But a church selection board turned her down. One member told her to return to the "peanut-butter-and-jelly ministry" of caring for her sons. So again Brenda put her dreams on the back burner.

A few months later, her husband's unexpected transfer to Long Island convinced Brenda that her time had indeed come. She applied and was accepted to the General Theological Seminary in Manhattan for a three-year master of divinity program. She commuted for a year and, shortly before her marriage dissolved, she moved into the seminary's living quarters with her sons, ages ten, seven, and five. It was a time of tremendous transition for Brenda and her boys. She admits, "I was scared to death. How was I going to study? I was thirty years old and not sure how my brain was going to function and absorb all this material. I was always a good student and I just hoped it was going to come back." Faced with a course load that ranged from theology and philosophy to ethics and liturgics, she pulled many all-nighters to get work done. "What saved me was the meals were included with the living quarters so I didn't have to cook," she says wryly.

Although she could have moved anywhere in the country she

decided to stay in the New York area and became a chaplain at two hospitals, a nursing home, and a retirement village on Long Island. Brenda offered spiritual and therapeutic support. "You don't just go in and hold the patient's hand. Talking to patients is sometimes like peeling an onion. You peel away layers to find out what their problems were. People need to tell their stories." The chaplaincy had flexible hours, so Brenda worked while her boys were in school and was able attend their many late-afternoon sports activities.

After five years, Brenda decided it was time for a change and moved to a parish with a three-hundred-person congregation. She reflected on the twists and turns that brought her to this point as a mother and a minister. Her boys are now young adults, and she firmly believes it was critical to spend those early years at home. She noted in an e-mail:

Staying at home with the boys taught me patience—more than I ever imagined I was capable of—patience which is grounded in love and care for those in my charge, a very necessary dimension to priesthood. Both the boys and those who are or have been my parishioners test it frequently! Staying at home with the boys taught me balance and perspective: when something was critical, like needing stitches, and when it was an ear infection that the doctor could take care of on Monday morning. This has been especially helpful in assessing situations with parishioners and various parish situations. Because, as you well know, the children and the parishioners all holler just as loud regardless of which it is—the stitches or the ear—but it is up to me to decide what's important and how to handle the situation. Staying home has also taught me humility, to laugh at myself, to place love as the highest priority—even above religion, and the significance of forgiveness.

Her life as a parish priest is fulfilling, and she calls it "a great privilege" to baptize, marry, and minister to her congregation. Any regrets? After overseeing a recent renovation of the church, she says ruefully, "They don't teach how to find a good roofer in divinity school."

Reigniting a Passion

Call it a passion or driving force. The name really doesn't matter, but if we didn't pursue this work we would feel that our lives were missing a vital component. Sometimes we follow that dream fresh out of college, plunging into work that consumes us; we don't mind working long hours and constantly being on call. Then along come children, and formula and wet diapers and the endless needs of babies douse that passion. So we happily succumb to motherhood and put our passion aside for a while. But it is always there, waiting for a time when life becomes a little more predictable. It's almost like we take that passion and cram it into a box, slam the lid shut, and put it away to be opened at some future date. Some of us pry open the box after years of planning and preparation. For others, the lid pops open unexpectedly, thanks to some chance encounter.

That was the case for native Californian Liza Wachter on whom serendipity smiled not once but twice. In her BC days, Liza worked as a corporate lawyer for a few years before finding a way to turn her passion for books into a job as an editor. When she had her first child at age twenty-nine, Liza put aside her work with the understanding that at some point she would return. "Even in my formative years I always knew that work would be important. I always had been pretty driven and ambitious about the things I love to do, and satisfying work was always my focus. Working with books and authors feels like a calling for me, like my destiny, and to not do it would make me feel like my life is incomplete."

In 1994 Lady Luck visited Liza for the first time as she pushed her son in a stroller along a shop-lined street in Pacific Palisades. She peered through a store window and saw a woman sitting on the floor opening boxes. Pasted on the window was a newspaper article about this new bookstore. Liza walked in, introduced herself to the owner, told her about her background and, voilà, was hired for a part-time job. For the next four years Liza sold books, arranged displays, and helped plan events, often with her two young children in tow. "The experience was wonderful because it was a baby-step transition back into the work world. It wasn't too demanding and it was all that I could handle at the time. It was actually a good experience for the kids."

Liza was forced off her feet during her third pregnancy and stayed home for more than a year. As her daughter approached her first birthday, and with the older children in school full-time, Liza began to think about going back. This time she wanted work that both nurtured her passion for books and carried long-term career possibilities. "With the kids getting older I realized I now wanted to get my career to the next level. It was just a feeling inside me that I wanted to make something start happening. While I loved being at the bookstore, I felt like it was time to do something that I could build upon." Liza was experiencing a feeling shared by many women. After quieting the biological clock, the career clock begins ticking progressively louder. If you hope to achieve a certain level of career success, then at some point you must stop thinking about it and start acting. That doesn't mean jumping right into a forty-hour workweek, but it does mean taking some measurable steps to start working toward that goal. Those steps include working part-time, going back to school, researching a career, or simply talking to people to gather information.

That was Liza's intent when she began meeting friends to pick their brains about the L.A. publishing scene. For one lunch date, she hooked up with veteran literary agent Sylvie Rabineau, who was about to start her own agency representing authors' dramatic rights. Lady Luck smiled on Liza again. By the end of lunch she had more than names to network; Sylvie asked Liza to join her as a partner in her new venture. "While starting my own business was shocking to me—I certainly hadn't planned that—it made sense, given our similar backgrounds and how they complemented one another." Sylvie also had two school-age children and fully understood that Liza needed time for the transition from family to work. And so the Rabineau Wachter Literary Agency was born.

Was this what Liza was looking for? Did it fulfill her passion? One summer afternoon she was sitting in the century-old Randolph Hotel in Oxford, England, with Philip Pullman, the prolific author of young adult books. Over tea, the pair discussed his acclaimed fantasy novels. "To me it was a dream to meet an author of this caliber. This is what I had worked for," says Liza. When she went back to her hotel in London she sat down with her older children, then nine and eleven, who had expressed unhappiness about Mom not being available every waking moment. "I told them about the tea and the amazing conversation with Philip.

'This is why I do what I do. It has always been a dream of mine,' I told them. I think when they saw how excited I was, they finally understood why I work."

Timing: Will It Ever Seem Quite Right?

Timing, in the sense of both your children and your career, is another variable in the decision to go back. The question that nags many mothers is how long to stay home. Through the infant years? Toddler and preschool? Primary grades? Once the youngest child is in school, the pressure builds for Mom to return to work. Part-time work often seems a solution. At least there's some income to help with expenses, and the part-time job lays the groundwork for returning full-time sometime in the near—or distant—future. However, some moms put off the decision to return because each year brings new challenges. "Next September" can be heard in households from coast to coast. After those physically exhausting years with toddlers and preschoolers, some moms just want a little break with time for themselves. They become involved in the schools and other volunteer work. Just when some moms are ready to return, the oldest child hits the middle school years, which some experts feel are even more critical than the preschool years for hands-on parenting. The timing never seems quite right.

That was the case for Mona Behan who was involved in her children's many activities. Because her husband was a photographer with frequent out-of-town assignments, Mona didn't want to commit to a full-time job. So she fashioned a freelance writing career, working from home. But nearly a decade in a home office began to lose its charm. "When I was at home I felt very isolated because a lot of my friends were working parents. I did schedule regular lunches and day hikes, but sometimes I'd feel guilty about taking that time for myself. I eventually realized that I needed the mental stimulation and camaraderie of an office."

Still, Mona was reluctant to leave her two teenagers. Most moms agree that it's when the children crash in the door at three P.M. that they get the scoop on what happened that day. But one winter evening, it dawned on Mona that it was six P.M., her children were at after-school activities, and she was home alone, as she had been every school day for months. "I suddenly realized that I was reduced to a chauffeur role and I didn't go to college to be a chauffeur. My children didn't need me in the same way they used to. I wasn't leaving them. They had left me and, in doing so, gave me the pathway to a new era of independence."

Other women, especially those with elementary school children, find that going to school themselves meshes nicely with their lifestyle. Everyone buys school supplies together; everyone is going to school; kids see Mom studying; Mom sees the kids studying (sometimes). Best of all, most degree programs offer flexibility in class scheduling so Mom can often be home by three P.M.

When Reverend Brenda Overfield embarked on a three-year master of divinity degree, her three boys were four, six, and nine. She originally had planned on waiting until they were older but changed her mind when she was accepted at a seminary. In retrospect, she is happy that she went to school at those middle ages. "Life is much more simple when kids are in grammar school rather than toddlers or teenagers. I could have waited, but I'm glad I didn't because I now see the turmoil of the adolescent years when they are much more at risk for making bad choices. At the middle ages they are in school all day and often at after-school activities."

Timing seems particularly problematical when children's ages span a decade or more. You stayed home with the older ones, returning to work when "the baby" started kindergarten. Suddenly getting to school events and volunteering for Brownies or soccer as you did for the older children is not so easy anymore. It's almost like you have a different set of mothering standards for the older children and the younger one. Yet after those years at home, time is passing and you must get going with your career again. That was the case for Elaine Levine of St. Louis, who started the long road back as a molecular biologist when her oldest two were in middle and high school and her youngest in first grade. Elaine needed a master's in biology to apply for the kind of research job she dreamed about, so the minute little Natalie went off to school, so did Elaine. But she still wonders, "One interesting question in my mind is that my three kids grew up in very different environments. For the oldest I was home, but there was not a lot of extra money; for the middle daughter, about half and half; and for the youngest I wasn't home all the time, but there was more money. There was a certain amount of guilt that I wasn't there when she got home from school but, yes, we can go shopping on Saturday."

There's no one answer to the perfect age. A lot depends on personal circumstances. Most moms we talked to did not want latchkey children. So the timing of going back can hinge on whether a school district offers an after-hours program or you can find a reasonably priced housekeeper or part-time day care. Maybe your husband's work finally offers him some slack so he can help out more. At Stanford Law School, Mary C. Baskauskas took a promotion to a full-time job when the youngest of her four children was twelve. It was doable because her husband works out of a home office and was willing to be the hands-on parent in the afternoon. "There was a sense that it was 'my turn' for a career, an unspoken agreement," says Mary. "We've always been a pretty good team, so when I was offered the job we made a joint decision of how we could make it work, and he was willing to pick up the after-school duties."

Children are not the only consideration when it comes to timing. If you want to go back to your old career and try to resume where you left off, the window of opportunity is not always open. Sometimes there's only a fixed period of time—often sooner than later—that reentry will work.

Kathryn Poling, a labor lawyer from Lorton, Virginia, knew that three to five years was the maximum time she could stay home before people who knew her work would begin to disappear. She met her husband when they were both working in a military legal office in Washington, D.C. Although Kathryn was a civilian employee and Dan was a high-ranking officer, he was still in her supervisory chain of command and they had to get permission to date. After a few dates, they were engaged within a week, and since Kathryn was forty-one when they married, the couple started a family immediately. Their game plan was for Kathryn to stay home when the family moved west for Dan's transfer and to return to Washington within five years so that Kathryn could go back to work. The plan "worked like charm," she says. Two sons were born during the three years that Kathryn stayed home fulltime. When Dan's reassignment to Washington was on the horizon, Kathryn started making job inquiries, expecting to return in a year or so. Her reentry was easier, and sooner, than planned—

seven jobs were available. As Kathryn notes, "Luckily, military labor lawyers are not a dime a dozen," and she was able to negotiate a very flexible full-time position, working a maximum of thirty-five hours a week. "I could afford to be choosy about the position because I really didn't want to go back to work just yet. However, I suspected this was going to be the ideal job for me once the children started school. I felt some compromises were in order." So she traded time for money. While she could have commanded a higher salary elsewhere, the Defense Department job gave her flexible hours: She is home by four P.M. every day and can take her son to nursery school several days a week. "I always knew that I wanted time more than money. Time is so important. The time we have with our children at home is gone in a blink."

Sometimes the timing has nothing to do with children or career. Look for signs. Sometimes they are subtle, like a neighbor seeking temp help during a busy season, and sometimes it's a big bang. For Doreen Lenichek from Los Angeles, the 1994 Northridge earthquake shook her up in more ways than one. A stay-at-home mom for fourteen years, the earthquake bolted her back to work in the L.A. County Office of the Assessor, where she had worked for ten years after college. Doreen recalls thinking, the morning of the quake, "This might give me work. This damage will need to be evaluated." Coincidentally, just before the earthquake she worked on a three-month project for the assessor's office, updating the square footage on commercial real estate. The temporary job convinced her that she could manage family and work. After working on the earthquake assignment for four years, Doreen was hired for a permanent position.

For Joan Waldman, who was away from teaching for sixteen years, it was a simple phone call one hot August day from a friend, an elementary school principal. There was a sudden opening for a math support teacher in his district. It was now or never. Joan jumped at the opportunity and now, eight years later, she is principal in that very same school in Rockville Centre, New York.

The lesson learned by Kathryn and Doreen and Joan, and scores of other women, is that the timing is never going to be perfect with all the ducks neatly in a row. Sometimes you need to plunge into the deep end of the pool and just start swimming. Eventually you will get to the shallow end where you feel safer. It may be a struggle, and you may even feel like you are drowning at times. Somehow it does seem to work out, that instinctively we decide what's important both in terms of family and career and what's not. And you won't have to worry anymore about your mind turning to mush because the wheels will be spinning constantly!

Money Can't Buy You Love, But It Can Buy You a Lot of Other Things

I took a part-time job at a much lower pay rate. In the long run it has worked out great. I love the people I work with, I have learned new skills, and have gotten other work opportunities as a result of taking this part-time job. I'm still not making the same salary as when I left the workforce, but I am much happier.

—Terry Nolan

Why do we work? Obviously for the money . . . the money for the mortgage or rent, the money for food and clothes and the car, the money for tuition and braces and vacation and, maybe, if there's any left over, for retirement. Of course it costs money to work, from commutation to clothes to child care. So just how much is enough? If someone dangles a $60,000 salary, it sounds great until you start to crunch the numbers. Our advice: Find an Internet site with worksheets for calculating your take-home pay after expenses and taxes. With the net income, you can make an informed decision about the financial rewards—or not—of going back.

Some women go back because they have no choice: Their husbands were laid off. Woman after woman in our survey noted that the downturn in the economy and the resulting job cuts propelled them back to work. One mom from Connecticut told us that she had always planned on going back but not until her youngest was well into high school. "It is a bit earlier than I wanted, but my husband has been out of work for a year and a half now. So I feel I had no choice."

One of the advantages of "keeping your hand in," as we discuss later in the book, is that you can pick up work more easily. Many women scoff at a part-time job because of the low salary. What they don't realize is that the real payoff comes with gaining experience they can parlay into better-paid work. That's what happened to Carolyn Hoyt of Tenafly, New Jersey, a freelance writer and mother of two girls. When the family needed additional income and health insurance, she called one of her magazine editors to ask for more assignments. To Carolyn's surprise, the editor had just accepted a new position at *Working Mother* magazine and offered Carolyn a part-time editor's slot. Carolyn's delight was tempered by her uncertainty. "I was completely scared to death leaving the house and the children and going into the city. I just wasn't set up to do this. But we had a clear and pressing need for money and health insurance so I took the job."

Other women return reluctantly because their husbands put pressure on them. Several women told us that their husbands signed on for a deal of "two people, two incomes" and find the burden of "three or four people, one income" overwhelming. One woman responded to our survey, "I really did not want to go back to work. I had seen one job opening and sent in my résumé. Suddenly my husband was pushing me to get a job." In some households an unspoken undercurrent surrounds every conversation about finances: "Money wouldn't be so tight if we had two incomes." While it is true there is a new generation of involved fathers out there, some men don't believe that 24/7 hands-on parenting is a necessity, or see it as a luxury they can't afford. Another woman who answered our survey wrote, "My husband is not very supportive of my decision to stay home and raise the children." The key word in that comment is "my," for as we have learned, the decision for Mom to stay home works only if both husband and wife agree. The flip side is also true: Going back has to be a joint decision. Some men like the idea of a wife taking care of the home front while they are out slaying dragons. A wife going back to work can upset the balance of power in a relationship. Some men are not cut out for Mr. Mom, even on a part-time basis. With other men, unless the wife's added income can pay for child care, cleaning, and grocery shopping in lieu of him helping out, there's trouble brewing in paradise.

The road back to work will have fewer bumps if the couple talks about possible scenarios. Carol Rolnick of Ellicott City, Maryland, found that compromise was needed when she wanted to return to work and her husband, an emergency room physician in Baltimore with long, grueling hours, preferred that she stay home to help care for their farm and horses. Carol, who has worked in varied jobs such as hospital administrator, dolphin trainer, and guidebook author, wrote in an e-mail, "I told Michael last fall that I had to have some sort of work, even part-time, preferably paid, that allowed me some intellectual stimulation and feeling of self-worth. I pointed out that both our kids were graduating from high school and needed me far less than earlier in their lives. He understood, and we reviewed a lot of possibilities. The decision came down to a compromise of sorts between my husband and me. He didn't want me to work full-time, as then things wouldn't get done around our five-acre place. (Like mowing!) Basically, he felt that he didn't need so much financial relief as he did the mental relief of knowing family and home were being taken care of." The solution: Carol found two part-time jobs, allowing her both to handle the farm with her children's help and get the intellectual stimulation she so desired.

For many moms, money is only one part of the equation. Our online survey found that women are looking for emotional fulfillment as well as income from a job, particularly the second time around. "I know this will be hard to balance—work and family," wrote one woman, "so I want to make sure that I will really love whatever job I take." Let's call it "job satisfaction." You must add that into the equation along with the money. Many women noted that if they go back to work in their forties, it is likely that they have still twenty years of work ahead. One mom wrote in her survey response, "I'd better make sure I enjoy it. When the nest is empty I can put more time into my work. It really needs to be something that will fulfill me."

While we may initially focus on the money as the prize, we often forget that that the money can fade into the background very quickly if we are not also rewarded with job satisfaction. "Most people first think of money when they appraise a job. Salary can overshadow other considerations for a while, but we know it cannot cure headaches, ulcers, and depression from working in unhealthy job settings," says Monica Schneider, a career counselor from Long Beach, California. "The coworkers, management style, and job-related circumstances are initially treated like accompaniments after looking at the salary and title of the job. But one to three months into a new job will reveal that the money is not the motivator. It is the daily, weekly assessment of satisfaction found in relationships and activities that determines much of our job satisfaction."

Often we find the job that provides the most emotional satisfaction also provides less income! Over and over in our interviews we heard the same message echoed: "The job may not pay a lot, but there are so many other rewards from it." There are several different ways to view your less-than-impressive income and still feel you are making a financial contribution to the family. One way is to regard the job as an investment in the future. When Mary worked as an adjunct, she deliberately never calculated how much commutation and the babysitter were costing because she suspected that she was probably losing money on the deal. But teaching was an investment—a way to "keep her hand in" so when the time came to return full-time she could successfully compete for a position. Just as you hold on to a mutual fund for the long term, evaluate a part-time job not only for the income but also for the potential payoff.

Ask yourself, "How much income do I need at this time?" If you are going back to work and your income is supposed to make a major dent in that $30,000 college tuition payment due next year, then the scales are going to weigh heavily on the income side. On the other hand, if your income is not needed for major expenses immediately, then you can consider instead a career's long-term investment potential.

Another way to consider how much income you need is to focus on funding one or two family expenses, like braces, summer camp, monthly car payments, or a contribution to a retirement fund. "Make an income goal," suggests Kathryn Sollmann, cofounder of Women@Work, a Connecticut-based organization that places returning professional women in paid internships that lead to permanent employment. "Instead of thinking that your husband's 'big' money will pay the mortgage and your 'small' money will buy little more than dry cleaning and groceries, assign a very clear value to the money that you will earn. If your money just goes in the pot anonymously, there's no visible value. But if you decide that your money will fund a specific expense, you can feel that you set and reached a goal and there will be no question that the money you earn matters. Decide what you want to fund and then what you need to clear after taxes to cover that expense. This gets women—and their husbands—thinking in a very positive new way about back-to-work income, rather than obsessing about the fact that they can't immediately return to their former income level."

The alternative approach is to consider what you will trade off for less money. Time for many women is as important as money and, in fact, could save money. For example, you can probably command a higher salary in a big city, but if you work in a suburb closer to home you'll save money on commuting, take-out dinners, and extra hours for babysitters and other expenses. Professor

Moen, in her Ecology of Careers study, found that "higher pay seems to be an incentive for a longer commute. Wives who commute longer have higher prestige, more income and more professional accomplishments but also experience less family satisfaction, lower feelings of success, and more spillover stress." So the question you must answer is whether the more lucrative job with a longer commute is worth the added drain on your time and extra expense. Again, don't simply stick your head in the sand; sit down with a calculator and crunch the numbers to see if you come out ahead or in the red! One university administrator, whose husband is self-employed, told us that the tuition benefits, generous health and retirement plan, and a fifteen-minute commute all make her "modest" salary a lot more palatable.

Some women view their job as "insurance" in case anything happens to their husbands. Kelley Senkowski of Byron Center, Michigan, had several reasons for starting her own travel agency, but her ability to be the family's main breadwinner was one of her concerns. "Owning my own business is comforting because what if something happens to my husband and I haven't worked in five years? This way I have peace of mind. I can bring my business up a level if I need to."

A career or a job? How old should the kids be? How much money do you need? Sometimes the answers to those questions seem to change by the minute and there's no particularly pressing reason to go back to work except that you've been talking about it for months—or years—and now you finally want to take action. So what should you do? Buy the best debutante ball gown you can fit into, throw yourself a coming-out-of-the-house party, and announce to family and friends that you're entering the work world? But wait a minute! When people ask, "And what are you going to do?" suddenly you're not sure what to answer. So forget the frock, scratch the party, and instead sit down with your agenda and sketch out a plan.

How Much Money Do You Need?

- Calculate your net income after taxes, child care, commutation, clothes, cleaning services, take-out meals.
- Figure how much you can save on those costs if you telecommute or work compressed hours or job-share.
- Working closer to home may mean a lower salary but more time and substantial savings in expenses.
- Look beyond salary at total compensation. Some benefits, like health care, life insurance, a prescription drug plan, 401(k), a computer, car allowance, cell phone, or tuition remission, may be better than straight salary.
- Consider the long-term payoff. A low-paying "starter" job often paves the way for more lucrative opportunities.
- Earmark your salary to cover a particular expense like the electric bill or car payments.

Recharge Your Career or Begin Anew?

I have been trying to go back to work for about two years. I quit my job (as a copy editor) about five years ago, after my first child was born. (I have two.) When I left, my boss and the editor who hired me told me I'd always have a job when I was ready to return. So I left work fully believing the myth that a woman can take time out from working to raise her children, and then return at the level at which she left. But I am finding that the myth is truly only a myth.

In order to stay somewhat competitive and professionally active while I wasn't working, I took a volunteer job and I took a class. But in the past two years, I have either had no response to résumés, or a form letter thanking me for my interest. My former bosses have since moved on, and the person I was in touch with recently from my old job said she'd consider me for an assistant's job. I feel that since I have been out of the workforce for five years, I am now faced with a choice of starting over as an editorial or news assistant—alongside the 21-year-olds—or switching careers.

—a mom's letter to Mary and Loretta

The harsh reality is that you can't just pick up where you left off. While you don't expect your old boss to keep your seat warm, many women are surprised to find that potential employers brush off all previous work. The hard-won experience gained in your ten years or so working BC suddenly seems to disappear. The reason, the experts tell us, is that the "ideal" employee works nonstop from college to retirement. "I think any mother who takes time out of the workforce faces significant struggles to go back," says Professor Joan Williams, director of Worklife Law at American University's Washington College of Law. "If workers take a sabbatical then they don't fit the model of an ideal worker. The assumption also is if you're out of the workforce it shows a lack of commitment and lack of seriousness. You're judged by the gold standard of the ideal worker, and that ideal worker doesn't need to take any time off because typically it's a man supported by a wife at home."

Of course there are ways to keep your skills updated and your résumé reasonably current. However, first you must consider a basic question: Do you want to go back to your previous career even if it means a lesser position and lower salary, or do you want to begin anew in another career? Think of your career as a hike in the woods; you just reached a fork in the trail. Now what to do? Take the new path or continue along the same trail? That new path might require additional training and schooling and the climb may be steep at times. Perhaps all you know is that you don't want to resume your BC career, but you don't have a clue what to do with the next twenty years (or more) of your work life. Maybe you like to make silk flower arrangements or play tennis or plan dinner parties or volunteer at the soup kitchen. It's doubtful that you can make a full-time career out of any of those avocations. So how do you decide? You could go to the library and check out the numerous books on careers and changing your life. You could take a battery of personality tests like the Myers-Briggs Type Indicator to discover what occupation seems a natural match for your innate traits. You could even hire a career coach who will steer and cheer you to a winning job. Perhaps you're not quite ready for any of those routes so to get you started we have done the legwork for you. We talked to career counselors from around the country who offer advice, from the basic to the advanced, on how to decide which path to take for the next twenty or thirty years.

To start with, don't be afraid to pick people's brains. Ask everyone you meet, from women waiting to put their kids on the bus to people socializing at your husband's business events. Make every meeting count. Make every chance encounter meaningful, even if it's just getting your name out there. Patti Branco, the owner of a management and training solutions firm in Southern California, encourages women to begin exploring careers by speaking with friends and acquaintances who have successfully returned to work. Don't be afraid to use the six-degrees-of-separation approach and call your neighbor's cousin's aunt who runs a catering business. The important point, says Patti, is to seek women with a positive frame of mind. "No whiners allowed," she says.

Another approach that does not require a major commitment is to "shadow" a person who has your dream job. No, we're not talking Katie Couric. Suppose you've been an avid *ER* fan for years and think that emergency nursing seems like a rewarding career. Before you enroll in Biology 101 at the local community college, try shadowing a nurse, suggests Karen Sutton, director of Continuing Education at Vincennes University in Indiana. Karen has counseled many moms returning to work and says that the flexible hours and good pay make nursing particularly attractive. However, after trailing a nurse for a shift, many women change their minds. "They don't realize that a nurse is on her feet all day, that she has a lot of stress and patient interaction, that she must often relay bad news, and deal with family members who don't understand. Many women just see a clean white uniform and $40,000 or $50,000 a year."

Mary, in her work as a journalism professor, meets college students who dream of becoming fashion magazine editors. As with any career, there are years at the bottom of the ladder. One student took Mary's advice to shadow an assistant editor, and after a day of checking prices on blouses featured in a fashion spread, the student declared, "If calling Bloomingdale's to check on prices is how I'll spend a year or so paying my dues then I don't want to do it." Better that she knows now than after she gets the job. Conversely, another student, after spending a day with a newspaper reporter working on a frenzied deadline, was excited by the demanding atmosphere of a newsroom. The lesson is not to rule anything out—or in—until you experience it firsthand, and shadowing is an ideal way with little investment of time.

The next step, recommended by many career counselors, is to make a "time line" of your life. Get out that agenda. Draw a line starting with your birth, ending with the present, noting significant events along the way. Find a quiet place to think this through; it's too important to do while watching soccer practice. The time line exercise is often used by clients of Crisanne Kadamus Blackie, managing director of career coaching and counseling at Promising Futures, in Falmouth, Maine. "Think about milestones, the important events in your life both positive or negative. The negative might be that you failed a course. Consider whether that is likely to happen again and what you learned from the experience. Look for patterns in both the positive and the negative; maybe you didn't realize that you are always a leader in a group. Then write about your experience. Look for some kind of thread. Maybe over the years you've always done some kind of sales. Maybe there's a passion in there not acknowledged."

As we start to mull over what we want to do with the rest of our lives, we sometimes do a time line in an informal sense. When Carol Rolnick decided to look for part-time work, she thought about her previous careers. She ruled out returning to hospital administration. "I'd be competing with people who are getting out of grad school. Employers were not interested that I was good twenty years ago. I also couldn't get enthused about writing grants or reviewing proposals. I'd have to start all over, and I just didn't want to." Carol thought about what she had enjoyed most at her various jobs and recalled that she always liked history and research. When writing *Wish You Were Here! A Guide to Baltimore City for Natives and Newcomers,*[3] she "loved ferreting out details and spending hours and days tracking original documents to find answers." While doing research for a novel she was writing about a Civil War nurse, she visited the National Museum of Civil War Medicine in Frederick, Maryland, and was fascinated. She asked about a part-time job. There were no openings, but she learned that all the paid staff had started as volunteers. So now she works as a volunteer "master docent," transcribing the 1864 diary of a Union assistant hospital steward, and she researched and wrote outreach presentation materials on such topics as medical myths of the Civil War, the foundation of emergency triage, and Civil War prison conditions.

That museum work certainly met all the intellectual requirements, but Carol also wanted a paying job that would help her "actually make a difference in monthly expenses and budgets." Again, instinctively doing a time line, she thought back to her favorite job as a dolphin trainer at the National Aquarium in Baltimore. She called a friend who had just rejoined the aquarium education department. Her networking paid off, and she was hired as a guide for behind-the-scenes, in-depth aquarium tours on sharks and dolphins. It took two jobs and a lot of time and effort to make everything fit together, but Carol is now happy with her work.

Crisanne Blackie works with clients who are "outplaced" by companies closing or downsizing. "One of my outplacement clients wrote on her time line that the most exciting time in her life was the year she spent in Paris during high school. This woman, previously a receptionist, was a fantastic artist and in her glory in Paris." After completing her time line, the client decided to follow her passion and started a small business designing and painting murals for children's rooms. "She's not making a lot of money but she is doing something she absolutely loves," Crisanne says.

The goal here is self-exploration rather than finding answers. Don't be surprised if the process takes weeks or even months. You may need to reexamine the time line over and over before a light-bulb goes off and you detect a pattern or strength. That's precisely what happened to Monica Schneider when she hit a career road-block. One picture-perfect fall day, Monica sat at a patio café at California State University in Long Beach and shared the round-about tale of how she ended up teaching students how to make career decisions. With striking red hair and a bright pink sweater, Monica radiates the enthusiasm of a cheerleader when she talks about career possibilities for moms returning to work, using her own life experience as an example.

Always interested in helping others, Monica received her college degree in occupational therapy (OT) and worked in the field until her husband, an army officer, was stationed in Germany. In Germany she could not work in OT and faced a void as to what to do with her time. "There was no one to counsel me, so I decided to counsel myself," Monica says with a laugh. She got a degree in counseling through a college program offered on the army base. When her husband was transferred back to Oregon, Monica decided to give OT another try. At first she was delighted working in a medical facility, even continuing part-time through the births of both sons. But an internal transfer changed everything: a new boss, new coworkers, and a different type of patient. Suddenly Monica was unhappy with her daily routine. Viewing her work through the lens of what she learned in counseling, she realized that the "job setting" might be the problem.

The job setting, she explains, is not just the physical location of your office, it's also the type of interactions you have with coworkers and your boss, with the clients or customers, even with the pace of the work. "The new position, even though it was the same type of work, was such a poor fit that I left under duress. But I searched out what was wrong with this picture and I suddenly realized that I had a disconnect with the setting of my chosen career." So Monica decided to put her new degree to use, and for the next decade she ran a part-time counseling practice out of her home. "It was a big challenge but also a blessing in disguise. I met hundreds of women in the same predicament that I had been in and it was very gratifying to help them make career choices."

Everything changed when the family moved to Southern California in 1993 where Monica's husband started his own business, and the boys, now in their teens, did not need Mom around as much. "When we moved I lost a lot of contacts and confidence. I had a renewed sense of conflict and discouragement. What do I do with my life now?" Realizing that she had reached yet another fork on her career path, Monica took her own advice and charted a time line and studied her life, her successes and failures, what made her happy and what didn't. "I realized that school has always been good for me and I have always done well with long-term projects." Suddenly that dream of getting a PhD in psychology did not seem so far-fetched. Hurdles—educational, financial, distance, and others—were in her way, but Monica managed to claw and climb her way over them. When it came to writing a dissertation, she decided to study that "job setting" dilemma she had confronted years ago. Her dissertation is the basis of the course she now teaches to college students trying to decide what to do with their lives. Although the material spans a semester, Monica, as we sat on the college's patio, was willing to distill the essentials of the course she had aptly titled, "Where Is My Coffee Cup?"

To begin, Monica suggests that you visualize yourself at work with a cup of coffee (or herbal tea, if you prefer). Think of what type of place might make you happy. Different job settings have different personalities, just like people. Questions to consider:

- Do I prefer to work alone, with other people, in a small office, or in a big organization?
- What kind of work do I enjoy doing: Is it fast-paced; is it a predictable routine?
- What about my hours? Full-time? Part-time?
- Why would an employer value me? What do I want to be appreciated for?
- What kind of job circumstances give me the most satisfaction: closing a deal, helping someone in need, creating a new concept, working with my hands, or doing a lot of talking?
- Picture a morning at a job. What is happening around me and what would give me a feeling of wanting to keep going?

As you go through this assessment, you may wonder about its usefulness. After all, you'll be lucky just to get hired. Can you really afford to be so picky about where you will work? Absolutely, if you want more from a job than a paycheck. If you are about to change your routine and your family's for a new job, isn't it crucial that you enjoy going to work? So get out your agenda again and start making notes. Writing it down is essential. Not only does it allow you to review and ponder your thoughts, writing it down is the first step to actually making it happen.

What's next? Take a look at your notes and see where you

might find some overlap between what you want and what actually exists in the work world. In her booklet, *Where Is My Coffee Cup? A Guided Search and Discovery of Your Preferred Job Setting*, Monica credits the notion of "congruence" to the "grandfather of career testing," John Holland, a John Hopkins University psychologist. "In 1954 he designed questionnaires around the belief that places of work had personalities just as people do. When we find a match between our personality type and the place of work, he called this congruence. Congruence would mean I am appreciated in my workplace, I bring a contribution, and the contribution is received with the exchange of job satisfaction," Monica writes.

Many of us consider congruence unconsciously. We dream about the kind of job that would make us happy. Some are pipe dreams; others are jobs that are within our reach.

We think about our personalities and talents. Remember your report card from elementary school? If you got an Unsatisfactory in "works and plays well with others," chances are you won't feel comfortable in a workplace that requires constant interaction. You might do better with something individually task-oriented. To find congruence you need to draw two circles. One is titled "This is me and what I want" and another "This is what is out there." Before Loretta went back to get her graduate journalism degree, she thought about congruence without even realizing it. First and foremost she wanted a job where she would continually be learning something new, a job that allowed her to interact with people from all walks of life, and a job where she could be creative. All those attributes would go in the "This is me" circle.

Loretta was not looking for an office-based job; the ideal position would be project-driven with flexible work hours. So in the "This is what is out there circle" would be different types of jobs that she might consider, such as a contract position, freelance work, consulting, and so on.

interact with people
be creative
flexible hours
contract work
investigative work

freelance journalism
ghostwriting
staff job
contract
corporate communications

THIS IS ME AND WHAT I WANT **THIS IS WHAT IS OUT THERE**

To overlap the two circles means you have found congruence. Don't be discouraged if the overlap is not extensive. Monica advises, "You have to realize career planning involves a lot of compromising. There is no perfect fit; congruence will come and go as your life changes. The best measure is that the work is congruent at least sixty percent of the time and that it can fluctuate with everyday circumstances. Some days might be actually greater than sixty percent satisfying." She readily admits that this soul-searching is not an easy task; she herself has done it several times throughout her life. Monica refers to the personality theories of Carl Jung. He believed that our psyche or personality develops and changes over the course of our lives. The "Self" as he called it, particularly in the second part of our lives, feels a "nagging demand to re-center our lives on a new, revamped set of values," she says.

When we first talked to Monica, she was in a happy, settled

place in her life. Then, as we were finishing this book, she wrote to tell us that her husband of thirty years died of a brain tumor in the summer of 2003. These new, unexpected changes in her life prompted her to consider once again the type of job setting that could result in congruence, matching her values and interests with her financial needs.

While she has made no decisions, Monica is considering a change to corporate training; it involves travel, which she had not previously considered. The courage to face the unknown with a less-than-precise image of what is ahead has been tested at least a few times. Monica explains, "What I have learned is to take the step to make something happen and another step will be revealed. They [the steps] do not all show up at the same time."

As Monica's case proves so poignantly, our lives take all sorts of unexpected twists and turns. Take the opportunity now to examine in depth what kind of work motivates and satisfies you. That soul-searching may be referenced again and again as life changes.

Stop Thinking and Start Doing

If you are still hesitant about making a career choice, starting school or part-time work, we have some advice for you: Just do it. There will never be a perfect time; some snag will always hold you back. The changes seem frightening. Let's face it: Home is safe and comfortable. You made it that way! If you go out into that brave new world you may have to talk to men other than soccer coaches; they may actually flirt with you. You will be expected to turn on the computer and know how to use it. You may miss a school concert and your child will be upset. But change should be familiar to you by now. After all, isn't a lot of motherhood adjusting to a series of changes? You can change a diaper with one hand in sixty seconds and suddenly they are potty trained. You finally get the names of the nursery schoolers right and then they're off to elementary school. One minute they want to hang out with you and the next they wish you were invisible. As our children change, we constantly reinvent ourselves, much more so than men. Think of going back as reinventing yourself one more time. Talk to yourself; give yourself the same good advice that you have given your kids all these years: Take chances. No pain, no gain. It's how you play the game, and so on. Those sayings may sound trite, but they do ring true. Follow your own advice.

One caveat: When you start to think about going back, don't make flexibility the only measure by which you consider a career or judge an offer. Obviously it's at the top of the list, along with money. But there are other factors. Pull out that agenda and make a list of all the pluses and minuses of a particular position, including such variables as opportunities for growing intellectually, being challenged by the work, broadening your social network, even job perks. What can be one mom's plus is another mom's minus. One mom might want to commute by car for convenience while another might relish the bus or train because it gives her time alone to actually read the newspaper or a novel. A part-time job at a bookstore might pay too little for one family, yet the same job works for another family because of the flex hours, discounts on books and gifts, and a place for the children to hang out.

While you are making that list, include your family members both individually and as a group. The pluses for your husband when you return to work might be an increased income, but the minus is that he will have to make dinner or assume some additional chores. The downside for your teenagers might be that you won't be available to drive here and there. On the other hand, you won't be hanging over the kids when they come home from school. They might even gain some increased responsibility. You get the picture. Take the time to write it all down and ponder it for a day or two. You should then have a better sense of the total impact going back will have on you and your family.

Two
Getting Going

WE'VE CONVINCED YOU. You've made the decision to go back, although you don't know when or where or what. Even with that uncertainty, you can be proactive, keeping your options open, exploring possibilities. Think about volunteering or going back to school or spinning off part of your former career. Staying home doesn't mean living in isolation, fully detached from the work world.

You may already be preparing to reenter without realizing it. The rules of staying home have changed. We don't know any moms who are watching soaps and eating bonbons. They are volunteering in schools and the community, getting stop signs erected, serving on curriculum committees, taking a night course at the local high school, running households like a small business, and guiding two—often three or more—children through the challenges and perils of twenty-first-century life. In other words, they are developing new skills and interests while at home.

The next step is to take those skills and interests and turn up the heat. How high you push the thermostat depends on a number of variables. You may have decided that you don't want to work at all before your children go off to school. In that case, use those at-home years to stay connected, sharpen certain skills, or even go to school yourself to learn something new. Maybe you can find a part-time job that is not demanding but helps you explore new areas.

You may be saying to yourself that's ridiculous, probably impossible. We are telling you that it can be done. For starters, when you receive the kids' school calendars, pull out your agenda. Start by giving yourself a first assignment. Write down a half dozen ways that you can keep your hand in the work world. If you are still staring at a blank piece of paper, don't panic. Here are some suggestions to keep up your contacts so your former colleagues don't answer "Who?" when you call. It's important to stay connected for networking down the road whether you intend to resume your old career or start anew.

How Can I Cut Out Paper Dolls and Keep Up My Business Contacts at the Same Time?

E-mail. Forget the excuses from days gone by. With e-mail it is so easy to keep in touch. You don't have to play phone tag or worry about twisting your words. You can keep your name or, better yet, your e-mail on the radar screen. But remember: Business e-mail is not for sending baby photos or sharing your kids' latest feats. If you can't think of anything to write, consider attaching an interesting article from a trade journal. Or forward a résumé suggesting a new employee who may interest your former company. Or why not send an e-mail asking your former boss for a special project? But don't go overboard; once every few months is enough to subtly remind former coworkers that you are still kicking. Another suggestion: Set up a separate "business" e-mail account. Forget about Stressedoutmom@, soccermom@, or prettylady@. These are fine for friends but will not impress anyone in the business world. Finally, make sure you keep the e-mail correspondence in a separate mailbox on your computer so you maintain a history of whom you chatted with, the dates, and the topic.

Find a mentor. We don't mean that you should call a former coworker and ask, "Will you mentor me?" Mentoring is an informal arrangement where you keep in contact with a coworker, usually one with some seniority, who admires your talents and work style. It's a given that we all like to work with people who are known quantities. So let this mentor know that you are available for smaller, limited projects. Even if you can't do that, make sure the person knows your long-term goal to eventually reenter the field. Keep in mind that people change jobs and get promotions. She may not need you at her current company but could call at some future date for another firm when you are ready to return.

If you must share mommy experiences, hook up with a former associate who is also a stay-at-home mom. Besides talking about teething and toilet training, you will inevitably get around to discussing office politics or industry issues. Form a mothers' group with women in the same industry and, although it might be more fun to meet monthly to discuss the latest novel, why not put business-related issues on the agenda instead?

Join a business association. Every industry has associations, many with regional groups. You may not go to the annual conference in Las Vegas, but you will be able to participate on committees and volunteer your services. Vicky Austin of San Francisco worked as a software consultant before staying home with her three sons. She joined a Women in Technology group to keep her contacts current. Through that grapevine, she heard about an opening for an adjunct professor to teach a software class at a local community college, and she grabbed the job. If there's no business association in your area, join any group that needs your business expertise. We know CPAs who advise their nursery school compensation committee. Vicky headed her local elementary school's technology committee and supervised the purchase—and installation—of dozens of new computers.

And make sure you get invited to the office Christmas party. Not only will it be an inspiration to start thinking about returning, but you'll also have an excuse to buy something other than jeans or jogging pants.

Volunteering

Unfortunately now that I would like to go back to work, at least on a part-time basis, my résumé's an outdated joke, and I'm fearful that business has probably changed so dramatically that I will be unable to adapt easily and will feel embarrassed and out of date. But God, I was good at PR.

—*Adria Rolnik*

Volunteer work can fill the big black hole on your résumé. It's perfect for women because it's the mother of multitasking. Think about it: You can "do good" for both your community and your career. Volunteering can mean anything from working the PTA car wash to serving as the regional chair for the Girl Scout cookie sale to working for a political campaign. Another plus is if you are willing to put in the time, you can move up the ladder fairly fast and attain a position of responsibility; that would be impossible so quickly in the private sector. Those contacts may pay off when you look for a paid position. However, when it comes to volunteer work, you must think like a man: Be picky! Have you ever met a man who volunteered to run the bake sale? No, the dads are running the golf outings or the capital campaigns for local hospitals. "The mother at home needs to think about building her résumé as much as a mother in the job market," says Professor Joan Williams, author of *Unbending Gender*.[1] "If you've been president of the PTA, it doesn't take a great leap of imagination for an employer to recognize that you have held an important leadership role. Take a lesson from men volunteers who most often assume leadership roles in volunteer organizations, the kind of stuff that looks good on a résumé."

That lesson was learned by a former actress and fashion show producer, Anne Moss, who has kept her foot in many doors over the last two decades. She carved out part-time gigs as a corporate spokesperson, TV model, and cable sports show host as her husband's newspaper publishing career took them from New York City to Miami to State College, Pennsylvania, to upstate New York. Yet it was her volunteer work in numerous community groups that eventually helped her land a full-time position as the executive director of the Community Foundation of Orange County.

One winter day, Anne, dressed in a trim blue business suit, sat in her Goshen, New York, office drafting a speech for an upcoming Rotary Club lunch, checking e-mail on one of her two computers, and deftly handling a local politician on the phone. "Let's all come to the table and have a very open and honest dialogue and talk about creative solutions," she told him. Anne's volunteer work, ranging from a child advocacy group to a college arts advisory board, prepared her to run an organization with a goal of raising $1 million annually. "Through that volunteer work I found a way to develop my skills and at the same time contribute to the communities that I lived in," Anne says. "This job sort of evolved from all that experience."

Anne had always intended to go back to work when her two children were in their teens, but getting back into fashion or television full-time meant a long commute to New York City and a fixed schedule. With two teens in different schools, Anne wanted more flexibility. Her volunteer efforts provided the answer. Anne was on an advisory board for the State University of New York at New Paltz when she was offered an interim position as a vice president of advancement, handling alumni relations, fund-raising, and communications. The job was full-time, including many nights and weekends, not exactly what Anne had in mind. But it was temporary until a new vice president was hired. "Those opportunities don't come along too often, so I thought I would do it in an interim capacity and see if I really am ready to do the necessary juggling to go back to work full-time," Anne says.

Her plan worked, giving Anne the "visibility" she needed. Several civic leaders were in the process of setting up a community foundation in Orange County, New York. Her community contacts paid off and Anne was offered the job as the first executive director. So why was she hired? "I think my organizational skills, communication skills, and understanding of nonprofit management and financial investment all helped me get the job," she says.

Make your volunteering count toward a real job and try to tie it into your career. If you're an accountant, run the PTA's finances; if you're a writer, volunteer for the school district newsletter; if you're an artist, design school murals; if you have an MBA in marketing, help with membership drives at your local synagogue or church. You get the idea.

Perhaps you are not sure that you want to go back to your former career. Then volunteer work can help you explore different areas, discovering your strengths and interests, some you didn't even know you had. Kathi Morse, a clinical social worker who specializes in bereavement and trauma, credits volunteer work with the Long Island Junior League for opening a whole new world. Kathi admits with a laugh that she had never even heard of "social work" before she volunteered as a family court special advocate, working with children. "My husband was constantly telling me that I had a head for business because I was so organized. Other people too just expected that I would go into business when I went back to work full-time." The family court experience spurred Kathi to seek a degree in social work, paving the way to her current job. The obvious lesson is that volunteer work can serve many purposes, including career exploration. Try a volunteer job outside your comfort zone, perhaps working with the elderly or joining an activist organization or mounting a Web site for your school. You may be surprised to find a new career.

Another approach is to think of volunteer work as nonpaid work. Often you can assume a position of responsibility as volunteer a lot faster than as a paid employee. Suppose you head a community committee. Chances are you'll work with government officials, local lawyers, businesspeople, and educators. All those contacts will help build your networking base that you'll need down the road when you go back. You won't just be another face either. Undoubtedly you will have impressed them with your intelligence and work ethic!

Another way to view volunteer work is to consider trading your time for on-the-job training. Many employers would consider that a bargain. Think beyond hospitals, schools, and government. Many private companies might consider a volunteer; you'll never know unless you ask. That's exactly what happened when Shirley Perlman, of Yonkers, New York, decided to go back. The mother of three adolescent children, Shirley had thought of several options for going back, including working at an advertising agency not too far from her home. One day after an interview for a copywriting position (she was offered the job but hated the product), she drove past the office of a weekly newspaper founded by Walt Whitman in 1838. On a whim, Shirley stopped the car and went in and introduced herself to the editor. She says, "I hit it off with the editor, a crusty old Brit and a terrific newsman, and I liked the feel of that little newspaper office." Shirley had absolutely no reporting experience and offered to work for free if the editor would teach her the business. "I felt it was a good deal all 'round. I didn't feel I was worth a salary at the time because I didn't know anything, but I wanted to learn. I felt it was a deal the editor couldn't refuse." Within a year, Shirley graduated to a paying position as editor. She spent the next decade working there and at other publications before joining *Newsday,* a daily newspaper with a circulation of five hundred thousand. At *Newsday* she was promoted to the national desk and covered stories from the O.J. trial to Monica Lewinsky. Not bad for what started out as a "volunteer" job at a weekly newspaper.

Admittedly, there are volunteer positions that don't translate to paid work yet can be useful in other ways. Mona Behan was frequently called on to make presentations in her new job as articles editor at The Dr. Spock Company. She credits working on school site councils that handled issues ranging from technology to dress codes with helping her overcome her shyness. "I kept getting put on these committees and made chair, and they helped me grow socially. I learned how to control a meeting; they helped me in public speaking, which I avoided before, and increased my self-confidence."

Once you find volunteer work that you enjoy, commit to no more than one or two organizations. When people know that you can get the job done, you'll likely be asked to join numerous committees. Remember, you can just say no. We know more than a few women who ended up working more hours as a volunteer than in paid positions. "Spread yourself thick in a few places, not thin all over the place. Pick two commitments that have meaning rather than ten that don't mean anything," advises Pat Alea, a career adviser and coauthor of *The Best Work of Your Life*.[2] Pat is also a strong advocate of taking a proactive role. "Find an issue that interests you, call the local government office, and get yourself appointed to a commission or committee. Too often those committees are staffed by the same people year in and year out, so they are always looking for a new voice." The end result is that you not only help your own career, you also help your community.

HOW TO VOLUNTEER . . . AND GAIN WORK EXPERIENCE

- Choose organizations where you can get a leadership role.
- Lead activities where there's a bottom line: raising money, building a new facility, getting zoning changed.
- Look beyond schools to civic organizations where you will meet local business and government leaders.
- Find opportunities for public speaking; you'll gain confidence and get your name known.
- Use your former work expertise to balance the books, write a newsletter, organize a winter coat drive.
- Try your hand at new jobs to explore different career paths. Lead a book discussion group, work with underprivileged children, become an emergency medical volunteer.
- Network like crazy, building a list of eventual business contacts.

Going Back to School

You know one thing for sure: Ten years of being a sales manager or teacher or CPA was enough. When you go back to work you want to try something completely new, completely different. Across the country, thousands of moms are preparing to launch new careers by attending noncredit continuing education courses, computer classes, and graduate degree programs. Going to school meshes nicely with motherhood. Classes are held during your children's own school hours or at night when Dad is in charge. You get those brain cells charged again and make new friends, albeit sometimes much younger. You get to study for tests and write term papers! Seriously, those tests and term papers are usually the deal breaker when it comes to going back to school. The very thought of getting grades again sets off an anxiety attack.

For those who are lucky enough to meet someone like Karen Sutton, director of Continuing Education at Vincennes University, the transition back to the classroom is smooth. Her office at this southwestern Indiana college deals with twelve hundred students a semester, the majority of whom are over twenty-five. Karen outfitted her office with a couch so women can sit down and release their inhibitions. "Many women come in very insecure, with low self-esteem, centering their life on their husband and family. We talk about what they've done and work with them in selecting a major. I have seen personalities change. I suggest taking a course with a relaxed atmosphere like sociology and psychology with many classroom discussions because these women have a lot of personal experiences they can contribute to class."

Going back to school is the perfect filler for the gap on your résumé. Think of it as collagen for your career. If your last job was six years ago, a degree six months ago can go a long way toward filling that hole. "Education is about as close to a magic bullet as you're going to get to help you reenter the job market," says Nancy Collamer, a career counselor with www.jobsandmoms.com, a Web site for returning workers. "Courses show an employer that you're serious and that you're willing to invest in yourself and learn new skills. It gets you out of the house, it gives you structure, it's helpful being around other adults, and it's good for networking when you are job searching." Nancy speaks from personal experience. When she was a stay-at-home mom with two small children, she registered at a local college in a career assessment program. A lightbulb went off for Nancy as she interacted with women who shared ideas as well as fears. In her former human resources position, Nancy was always on the hiring side. Now she wanted to advise people who were looking for jobs. "It was during this time that I realized that I always loved the career-counseling part of the jobs I had done."

While we continually stress the importance of planning, we have to admit that Lady Luck sometimes plays a role. When Nancy decided to look for a graduate program in career development, she learned that there were only three such programs in the United States and one was located in New Rochelle, New York, a short commute from her home. That's what we mean by lucky. As the search for a school begins, it is important to be realistic. Consider school locations. You will be surprised that some city universities have suburban satellites. Don't set yourself up for failure by applying to programs that you are not equipped to handle because of a time commitment either in class hours or distance. If your children are still at home, you might want to think about weekend or evening courses when your husband is around to take charge. Start thinking in terms of the school year and semesters. This shouldn't be hard. You do it all the time with your kids. And finally, start out slowly. You don't have to begin with twelve credits. Begin with one course. Look at the size of the class and the support services available, like teacher-student advisement. Breeze through a bulletin from the local community college to see what sparks your interest, but please, please be sensible. Sure, you may want to be a rocket scientist, but if you never took a physics course it's unlikely that will happen.

For Nancy, a graduate degree was her passport to a new career. However, she is quick to say that school doesn't have to be synonymous with a two-year or four-year degree program. What if you don't have a college diploma? If you hated school when you were fifteen, it's unlikely that you will like it any better at thirty-five or forty. Many fields, from interior design to nonprofit fund-raising, offer certificate programs that can lead to satisfying jobs. There are more options out there than flavors at Baskin Robbins. For some it might be a continuing education certificate program to become a Web designer or wedding planner. For others it could be computer training at a temp agency or online education.

If you get sweaty palms at the thought of a test, consider programs that don't require entrance exams. When Loretta returned to school in her midforties, she enrolled for a master's degree in liberal studies, an interdisciplinary graduate program at New York University. Why liberal studies? It was the only graduate program she could find that did not require the Graduate Record Exam. At that point she was interested only in getting that long-coveted degree, having been a grad school dropout. As she got closer to completing the degree, she realized that she had learned about philosophy and art and literature but nothing practical to prepare her to launch a new career. The winter before she got her diploma, she applied to the graduate program in the Department of Journalism, which required the GRE. Since both journalism and liberal studies were in the same graduate school, Loretta hatched a plot: She would argue that since she was already in the grad school, moving from one department to the other shouldn't require the GRE. Maybe they took pity on her because she was an older student, maybe she was a fast talker, or maybe she really had a good case, but the GRE requirement was waived and Loretta was accepted into the journalism master's program.

An added benefit is that Mom going to school often has a positive impact on the family. During counseling sessions with students, Karen Sutton discusses how going back to school affects the family and children. "The children's view of education changes when Mom studies as well," says Karen. "They buy school supplies together and graduation becomes a family affair." Nancy Collamer adds, "My older daughter was just starting kindergarten and getting into the concept of school. She would grab my paper; it was almost camaraderie."

When is the right time to return to school? When the children are in elementary school? When they are teenagers? "I always say there is no time like the present; you are never too old to go back to school," says Karen Sutton. "Right now moms may have small children, but as kids get older the expenses get higher for car insurance and tuition. And while the children are home you might be more eligible for financial aid."

Many moms find that succeeding in school gives them the confidence boost they need to go back to work. When the youngest of her three sons started school, so did Kathy Scheller of Wilton, Connecticut. Kathy, a former bank executive with a BA in marketing, chose to fulfill a dream to pursue a medical career. At age forty-two, she enrolled—one course at a time—in a nursing program at a local college. It took five years to get through the basic science courses and two more for the advanced work. Slowly but steadily she did it, and Kathy started a nursing job in a local hospital in 2001.

The mother of two young girls in Washington state shared a very similar experience with Kathy. Donna worked seventy-hour weeks as a financial analyst for a Fortune 500 company and was "halfway" to an MBA in her BC life. Six years into staying at home, she hit a long winter that left her feeling "blah and empty." A doctor advised her to return for antidepressants if she was still feeling down in a few months. Instead of drugs, she too resurrected a deferred plan of being a nurse and headed back to school for biology and chemistry courses. "This winter season was fine. Things are too busy to say, 'Poor me, stuck in the house.' This is positive stress, and I'm getting A and Bs," she says.

Perhaps you find the thought of dealing with eighteen-year-olds on a social level appalling, or you can't even squeeze in a night class. Or a degree in dance therapy is not offered at your local college. For those who can't find their way to a conventional school, there are twenty-first-century alternatives. Try the Internet. You can do just about everything else online, why not go to school? More than two million students enroll every year in what's called "distance learning." Patricia Appleton lives in North Orlando, Florida, and she's working on a degree in information systems management from the University of Maryland. How does she do it? Online courses. Patricia, with a little help from her son, taught herself Web and software design. She originally went back as an active duty air force reservist, working as a planner for medical-training exercises. She now works as a systems developer for a software development company in Florida while taking four classes a semester online. She finds the workload manageable because she can tailor it to fit her hours and feels both better equipped for her current job and positioned to be more competitive in the future.

Don't snub your nose at online course work. You will be surprised how many interviewers will say, "Hey, how did you do that?" when they hear about an online degree. And don't think that it is an easy way out. If you are going for an online MBA, you might find yourself at the computer in a study group six or seven days a week and have more direct contact and interaction with your professor than in a large lecture class.

College professors often say that older students are better students because they know how to manage their time and keep their focus, viewing school as a window of opportunity. Still, many of us are downright scared. Granted, it's hard to start something new and it's harder still to switch gears from home to homework. Don't be surprised if you keep putting the application in the back of a drawer for weeks, months, or maybe years. A million and one thoughts will swirl around in your head before you are ready to lick the envelope. Will I have time to do the work? Will everyone know more than I do? How will my family react? Will I stick out among twentysomethings? Our advice: Be an optimist. Then just do it, heeding the words of career coach Crisanne Kadamus Blackie: "It is often easier to go back to school than to stay home."

For some of us, taking one course at a time is a major feat. Others are satisfied with nothing less than a Ph.D., law degree, or MBA, all of which require a tremendous commitment of time, money, and energy. Women trying to raise a family and earn an advanced degree face a very difficult task yet feel the payoff is worth the effort. It may take four or five or more years, but there's a diploma and a satisfying career waiting at the end. Suellen Mazurowski knows this firsthand. These days, you'll find her practicing law out of her office on the courthouse square in the small Midwestern town of Sidney, Ohio. The road from stay-at-home mom to self-employed lawyer was filled with potholes, yet Suellen will tell you it was worth the journey. The youngest of her three children was about to start second grade and Suellen was ready to go to school too. Always interested in history and politics, she spent a summer reading course catalogs looking for postgraduate work. Well aware of the kind of tenacity required, she signed up, at age thirty-nine, for the law school entrance exam. She settled on law school because, unlike some business degrees, she wouldn't need to go back to college for additional courses. That was the easy part. Then came the notoriously difficult LSAT. "It was scary. During the LSAT I went into the restroom and met another mother who said, 'What am I doing here? I have two kids,' and I thought, 'Yeah, and I have three.'"

Suellen was accepted at law school, went part-time over four years, and graduated in the top 20 percent of her class. But it was not easy. "The most challenging aspect is getting it all done. I couldn't really do all the reading. I had to listen to briefs on tape. It was physically exhausting with the business of raising the children at the same time. I often asked myself, 'Who did I think I was with three kids going into a demanding intellectual course of study?'" She credits a cooperative husband and children, who learned to be self-sufficient. "In many ways my law degree belongs to all of them," she says. Despite the obstacles, she pressed on and the reward was first a career in government and now her own practice where she is the boss. Her staff includes two paralegals, both married women who work part-time.

Keep in mind that while you may be energized by your new goals, some of your friends may pull away. You now have priorities other than the PTA and power walking, and that can cause some tension. When Monica Schneider of Huntington Beach, California, enrolled in a doctorate degree program in industrial psychology, her friends did not fully understand why she was devoting hours to research and term papers. "I began spending more time with my classmates for camaraderie and support. Sometimes I envied my friends' free time and other times I was glad I had this focus."

Monica does not paint a picture of an idyllic life in an ivory tower. She is honest and acknowledges that the course of study was difficult on several levels, from finding the energy to push herself to class, to studying after working part-time, to having confidence that she would complete the program. "I took some risk not knowing if it would come to fruition. What helped me was my determination to make something good come of this move and something good come from the difficulty of school. I also realized that this was my own individualized achievement and not dependent on anyone else." When things got rough, Monica visualized herself at graduation. That came true four years later, and now Monica teaches career counseling at the University of California at Long Beach.

For Monica, what helped maintain that determination was the realization that getting a degree was a long-term goal, not something that would be done in a year or so. Sometimes, though, it's the sense of urgency, of time slipping through our fingers that propels us. Former flight attendant Kathi Morse got her college degree over the course of eighteen years while raising three children. As soon as she graduated college, she enrolled in a full-time graduate program in social work. With two children in high school and one in college, she was determined to finish within two years. Even determination does not lessen the fact that school requires a significant commitment of time and our brain cells are not getting any younger. Many moms told us they locked themselves in a room one weekend day or stayed at school to study. It can be a daunting challenge to take on a strenuous course of study, as Kathi found. "I remember the first four weeks, every Friday night I sat in the driveway and cried," says Kathi. "I was scared and I didn't think I could do it. And I thought, 'I've set myself up to fail.'" Her daughter and her husband, Jack, took turns coming out to the car to tell her, "I know you can do this. Don't panic. It's going to be okay."

Kathi was suffering from a common ailment: perfectionism. She knew she was a good mother and wife and now wanted to be an equally good student. "I just didn't feel like I could do it all. And I was right, I couldn't and that's not me. So what Jack and the kids ended up doing was giving me permission to not be the perfect mother or perfect wife. They said, 'You just can't do it all so let go of some things.' I said, 'You don't mind?' And I remember feeling that sense of relief when they would say things like that."

Going back to school is also a little like being on stage. We're up there for everyone to see us succeed . . . or fail. There are grades every semester, and having made such a fuss about our children's report cards, it's not like we can ignore a C ourselves or easily dismiss a late paper. Kathi had those concerns too—"fear of being able to do the work, just fear in general of failing. I wanted to do this and nobody was going to stop me. And then it was like, 'Okay, everybody's watching now.' What happens if you don't pull it off?" Kathi did pull it off and landed a succession of social work jobs. She enjoyed her work so much that after five years she decided to go back to school a third time for additional certification. While working as a bereavement and trauma therapist, she found an excellent year-long, one-day-a-week certificate program. But it was in Boston, three hours by car from her home in New York.

Kathi followed a model we encountered many times. Moms test the waters, find they can swim, and then go farther and farther as their confidence and experience—and children—grow. That was the case for Kathi. Undeterred by the distance, she enrolled in the course, which meant driving to Boston on Sunday afternoon, staying with her son, attending class all day Monday, and then driving home. She cut her work hours to part-time at the Schnurmacher Family Bereavement and Trauma Center. All her plans were in place for the first session of the course, scheduled to start late September 2001.

Then came September 11. Thousands of mothers, fathers, sisters, brothers, cousins, friends, and other relatives were lost by families in the area served by Schnurmacher. Countless people needed help, from families who lost loved ones, to those who had barely escaped from the World Trade Center, to those traumatized by the terrorist attack. Kathi used everything she learned from her Boston class almost as she studied it, from individual counseling to group presentations. "From the time I walked in the door here on September eleventh, through the next year, I was on high run." Part-time ratcheted to full-time, but she still completed the trauma program. Obviously it was—and continues to be—an emotionally difficult job counseling the children and families of 9/11 victims. But for Kathi it was the culmination of all those years of school. "I feel that I was making a difference. Doing good."

Monica, Suellen, and Kathi all successfully used going back to school as the route to going back to work. If you haven't figured out your path yet, we urge you to keep thinking about it and start moving forward, even if it means taking baby steps. Listen to some advice from Kathi: "I'd say don't be afraid to take a challenge and try it on. The worst thing that could happen is that it doesn't work for you and then you try something else. I've seen too many people stop themselves from doing things for fear that they will fail. You need to reframe it and don't even worry about if you're going to fail or succeed. See what happens. Just do it."

DOS AND DON'TS FOR MOMS ON CAMPUS

- Don't pierce any body part but your ears.
- Don't try to look like the others. You may buy your clothes at J. Crew, but you're not a campus co-ed.
- Don't be a know-it-all.
- Don't say, "When I was in school . . ." Nobody cares.
- Do learn computer skills before you go back to school.
- Do use the same tactics with fellow students that you use with your kids: compliment and build confidence.
- Do start slowly with a course or two.

New Takes on Old Careers

If you are totally baffled about your future career plans, consider putting a new spin on your old career. You have education and experience in a particular field. Unless you abhor it, why not pick the parts that appeal to you and construct something new with the pieces? Think about what you did BC and rework it, extract from it. Like TV shows, some careers lend themselves to spin-offs more than others. But how do you do this? First look at your field from a macro, not micro, point of view. Take technology, for example. We found women who were computer software specialists and turned that experience into part-time careers teaching at local colleges, working in public relations for high-tech companies, and consulting. Ellen Lawrence, a former research scientist for Monsanto in Missouri, with a Ph.D. in mycology plant pathology, started her own business as a technical headhunter. Sheila Ballard, a former auto insurance adjuster from Mount Laurel, New

Jersey, became a field representative for a company that inventories used cars and their condition.

Even fashion careers can be repackaged. While buying curtain fabric one day, Mary chatted with the saleswoman who saw her part-time job as an unofficial "internship." She had been a dress designer BC, traveling to Paris and Milan. Now she was learning interior design and "practicing" by helping customers choose fabrics. (By the way, her suggestions were perfect.) Just like this budding interior designer, take a look at the big picture of your interests and categorize them into the broadest possible field and then start extrapolating from there. Try this: BC you were a breast cancer researcher with a degree in biology. Now you have two boys, who love to do science experiments with you at home. What kind of work could you craft for a woman with these credentials? Meet Christy Ahsanullah.

As a researcher at the University of Texas Southwestern Medical Center in Dallas, Christy was responsible for examining an enzyme that is a marker for the presence of breast cancer in postmenopausal women. "That little enzyme can do a lot," she said. As important as her work was, Christy, mother of two small boys, soon realized that she couldn't be a full-time researcher and mom. Research often requires weekend hours if tissue needs to be immediately examined. For a while, she considered becoming a pharmacist, but those hours were often unpredictable as well. So Christy took the macro look at her field and came up with a creative solution.

As an at-home mom, Christy has spent hours doing science projects with her small children, from growing tadpoles into frogs to collecting bugs. Slowly it occurred to her that other children might benefit from the science "lessons" that she had been giving her sons. About the same time, she had enrolled at a community college in a class on starting your own business, thinking that might provide some possibilities. The two ideas collided and a business was born: Christy could earn an income teaching science to children.

Who would believe that preschoolers could be taught about gravity, momentum, and ecolocation? Christy does, teaching science at a local recreation center with projects and games like musical dinosaurs, her own version of musical chairs. She teaches in six-week blocks, two days a week, ninety minutes for each class. "It's an awful lot of work and I don't make enough—$6 a child for one and a half hours—and I pay for materials. But it's money to buy my kids whatever new things they want." Christy now gives the same course at a second recreation center. Her professor in the small business course became her mentor and cheerleader, pushing her to create her own Web site and brochure. "I was thinking that I should send the brochure out, but I want to grow slowly and I don't want to get so big that my children suffer," she says.

Often we heard from women who want to go back to their old careers but haven't kept pace with the changes in their fields. That didn't stop Susan Seigel, from Freehold, New Jersey, a former research assistant in microbiology. Susan decided to become a high school science teacher, so she went back to school to get her education degree and brush up on her science. Don't think that she didn't consider going back to the lab. On the contrary, she loved it. But the laboratory and family may not be compatible. "You can't leave an experiment to go to the soccer game," says Susan.

Teaching in a magnet medical sciences program for gifted students, Susan has a biochemistry class where the students do their own research projects. In fact, some have even won prizes for their work. Susan's worry about the classroom was that she would miss the highs that she had working in the lab on such virulent organisms like *E. coli*. "The kids are wonderful because they come up with amazing ideas," she says. "I miss the discovery, but I have that now with the kids. I see their faces light up with each discovery."

Maybe you want to work at home but are unsure about what sort of business you could run. Think about becoming a consultant, using the knowledge of your former field. You have the contacts, the network, and the information (even if it is dated). What's the worst thing that can happen? You won't get any business? You already have a phone and computer, so the start-up costs are minimal. It just takes some creative thinking about how to spin your old job into a new at-home business. Annette Herbert of Milwaukee had been a shoe buyer. How to flip that into a home business? Annette's first job out of college was with Mason Shoes, a major shoe catalog company in Chippewa Falls, Wisconsin, and her second was with Kohl's department store. Although Kohl's provided on-site child care, Annette felt that her ten-hour days were too long for her two small children, so she resigned. When her daughter entered kindergarten, Annette faced the familiar "Now what?" She didn't want to work full-time. Mason had urged her to return if she ever wanted a job again, but the company was located too far away to commute. Undeterred, she called her former boss and proposed a fifteen-hour-a-week contract position working on whatever projects they needed done.

She works out of her home, contacting vendors for various catalogs. The arrangement benefits both Annette and the company. "Why hire me?" says Annette. "I know the company, know its background, and know their customers. They know me and they trust me, and there's a lot of trust involved. If I tell them I worked ten hours, they need to believe I did, and I do. I accomplish a lot in two- or three-hour spurts. I am not chitchatting with other workers and I am very productive."

With two young children and at age thirty-four, Annette is not overly concerned with where the job will lead. "My husband says it is keeping my foot in the door and that perhaps I could get more clients and end up doing this full-time. I haven't thought that far ahead. It could help me get a full-time job if I chose." A lesson learned from Annette's experience: Always try to leave a job on good terms. As much as you might be tempted to tell your boss what you really think of him or her, don't burn any bridges. You never know when you may need those connections again.

The trick is to take your talents and skills and fashion a job that works, part-time, full-time, at home, or in an office, for your particular needs at a particular time in your life. We know lots of moms who tutor math, English, SAT prep, or a foreign language. We've met accountants who work only during tax season and lawyers who do only house closings. Often the challenge is to jettison the part of your old career that no longer appeals to you—an aspect of the work, the industry, the pay, the hours, or all of the above—and to use what's left to start a new career.

That was the dilemma confronting Sheryl Stern who had spent more than two decades working as an advertising art director before a long struggle with infertility ended happily with two children.

While her children were little, Sheryl continued to freelance as an illustrator. Work was in her future, but what kind of work? "Advertising is very high-pressure and heartless. I knew I was looking forward to a career outside my home when the time was right. I wanted to combine my interests in art and psychology and do something that helped people." Sheryl had been a psych minor in college and obviously has an aptitude for art. A career as an art therapist seemed to check all the boxes on her list—art, psychology, and helping other people—so she enrolled in a master's program.

Sheryl is similar to so many of the other women we talked to in that she did extremely well academically in the program, a classic older student. She started a part-time job two days after she graduated, working in an outpatient clinic treating people with eating disorders. It was an ideal job, combining all her passions. Sheryl would still be there, if the hospital hadn't merged with another and closed the clinic.

Now she runs a private practice where she uses art therapy to help treat people suffering from depression, stress, sexual abuse, infertility, and marital troubles among other problems. She also teaches college courses to other art therapists and has illustrated a children's book about attention deficit/hyperactivity disorder. With all this, Sheryl is still home by four P.M. for her two teenagers because she believes it's critical "not so much for keeping them in line as to be there when they have a bad day or great day."

Again like other returning moms, Sheryl is so energized by her second career that she has started work on a doctorate. She adds, laughing, "Some of my friends say I do way too much, but I see so many areas of interest that I would love to research as a way to continue to help others." And there's no end in sight for her.

Sometimes you may want to stay in your original field but not at the same level of intensity. You don't want to travel cross-country or work sixty-hour weeks. You proved you could climb the career ladder once. This time around you are more interested in that elusive work-family balance. Take advantage of your high-powered experience and trade it for flexibility at a organization that will be delighted to get someone with your credentials. When she started her journey back to work, Robin Edwards knew she wanted something different from the years she spent recruiting newly minted lawyers for one of the world's largest law firms. Robin had worked through the birth and early childhood of her two children, moving from one firm to another, until at her last job she had a staff of eight reporting to her. A series of events convinced her that it was time to leave when her children were seven and twelve. For the next six years she threw herself into parenting and the PTA. When her daughter started college and her son entered eighth grade, Robin, at age forty-eight, decided to look around for a new job, maybe in nonprofit, maybe in academics, but definitely not a major law firm. "I didn't want the intensity of a big corporate organization," she recalls. "I wanted the stress level lower and something a little more family-friendly. I didn't need to be boss but I didn't want to clock in and out either."

One Sunday, while reading the newspapers, she opened to the classifieds and on a whim looked under "law." A listing for the New York County District Attorney's office caught her eye. The DA's office prosecutes criminals, works closely with police, and pays less-than-stellar salaries. "I read the ad and thought,

'This is the job I want.' First, it's a whole different area, government and criminal law. And while the bare bones outline of the job would be the same, the routine of recruiting for a DA's office was very different than a Wall Street firm. I'd be seeking a different 'profile' of lawyer. But the only question is, 'I am really old; are they going to want me?'"

It turned out that the main concern was whether Robin could handle the New York City Criminal Courts Building, sharing the elevator with prisoners in handcuffs and scruffy undercover police officers, a real-world *Law and Order,* not the sanitized TV version. "So before I was offered the job they had me come downtown and walk through the halls and courts and the metal detector. My predecessor gave the tour and I thought it was so different and so alive. There's so much going on and it's so stimulating."

Three years into her new job, Robin is still energized by the work. She finds that both her prior experience and her time at home have combined to help her work more effectively. "It's easy to do a good job because of all the prior experience. I don't stress about the small stuff, and everything is not a crisis. I am mellower. If I had worked straight through, I don't think I'd feel that way. It's a shift in the way I look at life. I also think that before, I never considered quitting because I always feared I would never get another job. Now that I have this it's calming. I don't have that worry anymore."

Apparently her age was not an issue. By coincidence, the woman she replaced was leaving to stay home with her two children. Robin recalled, "I later told her that I was concerned about my age. She said, 'We never looked at it. We looked at your experience.'" Even with six years at home, Robin's considerable experience in the private sector was "valued-added" for the government position.

OPEN A DOOR TO A NEW CAREER . . . OR YOUR OLD ONE

Accept an interim position as Anne Moss did as a vice president for fund-raising and communications for six months

Take two part-time jobs rather than one heavy-duty full-time job as Carol Rolnick did as an aquarium guide and Civil War museum docent

Take a part-time job that might be compatible with a job you want in the future as former editor Liza Wachter did when she worked in a bookstore before becoming a literary agent

If someone asks, "Do you know someone who can do this job?" suggest yourself as Staci Handschuh did when the local police chief asked her to recommend a community youth center director

Take an alternative position as a stepping-stone as elementary school principal Joan Waldman did when she took a job as a math support teacher in two different schools

Trade on-the-job training for pay as Shirley Perlman did working for no pay at a small-town newspaper to learn reporting

Go back to school . . . slowly as former banker Kathy Scheller did, taking seven years to get her degree in nursing

Enroll in a graduate program as Suellen Mazurowski did when she started law school the same year her youngest went to second grade

Start slowly with a part-time job as Candace Hill did in a bookstore during the holiday season

Create a new career based on your old career as former cancer researcher Christy Ahsanullah did when she started teaching science to preschoolers

Three

Work That Works

Interior law office—day.
The camera zooms in on an office door that says:

LINDSAY DOLE, ATTORNEY AT LAW
MOTHER

LINDSAY: I want to start my own practice. I can take collection cases, contract disputes . . . (*Lindsay looks at the office door. To colleagues:*) Don't you like it?

ELLENOR: Usually the personal stuff is left off the door.

LINDSAY: I will take it off eventually, but I want people who hire me to get the idea I'm not going to stay late or be on call at home. When they see "Mother," it makes the point.

—opening scene, *The Practice*[1]

THE QUESTION, "WHAT DO WOMEN WANT?" might have tormented Freud, but the answer, according to our survey results, is flexibility (other than twenty-four hours alone). Whether they intend to go back part-time, full-time, or some arrangement in between, most moms want some give in their work schedule so they can be home when the kids walk in the door, or come in late if Grandma has a doctor's appointment, or work at home on a snow day, or maybe even enjoy a long lunch with some girlfriends. They want that flexibility without having to look over their shoulder or make 101 excuses or pretend to be sick when it's really Susie who has the stomach virus.

How can we be there for our kids, for those special moments, for life's watershed markers, and still go back to work? Flexibility is the simple answer. Hundreds of women who answered our survey felt so strongly about flexibility that many took the time to write an additional comment. "A flexible work schedule is the biggest challenge I see right now. My engineering career included many long hours and very rigid schedules," wrote Julia King of Zionsville, Indiana, a former senior project engineer. "The primary reason I have returned to school to study human resource management is a hope for a more flexible, part-time position when I reenter the workforce. If employers truly want to attract and retain talented women employees with young children, flexible schedules need to be integrated into the workplace as a top priority."

Unfortunately, it has taken decades for American business to hear women's screams for change. The good news is that slowly companies large and small are beginning to understand that to lure and keep the best employees they need to change their set-in-stone ways of viewing the ideal worker as someone who is on-site nine to five, five days a week, and then some. "Flex hours are not a gift to an employee," says Dr. Diane Halpern, president of the American Psychological Association. "It means fair wages for a certain number of hours. Companies will learn that it is in their financial interest and workers must demand it."

You are not alone if you shudder at the thought of being a nine-to-fiver again. More than fifty percent of workers want more flexibility in their work hours, according to *The Wall Street Journal*.[2] The message is that employers need to offer flexible work arrangements where work time is not measured by face time. The argument is that their worth should be based on the quality of their work rather than the hours in the office. Just because your boss can't see you doesn't mean that you aren't working. Another mom who answered our survey wrote, "People just need to allow women the flexibility to get their job done and trust that due to the flexibility they will get the job done and do it right!"

While many organizations keep workers tethered to the office with cell phones, BlackBerries, and beepers, others have finally realized that communication can be two ways. Sometimes it doesn't matter whether the vice president of marketing is pounding away on the computer in the office or at home. Sometimes it does. One executive at a Fortune 500 company says, "Big negotiations in person are becoming a thing of the past. It's e-mail, phone, and teleconferencing. The need for people to be in one place—all together—has been significantly reduced. In the last five years, I've experienced—even with men—their willingness to be on a business phone call while simultaneously talking to their three-year-old who wants Daddy to hang up. All of this is becoming much more acceptable and appropriately so."

Contrary to popular belief, the recession has not taken a toll on corporate work-life programs. Hewitt Associates, a global outsourcing and consulting firm, recently surveyed 945 major companies and found that "soft" benefits were not eradicated because times are tough. Nearly 75 percent of the businesses surveyed offer flexible work arrangements, 59 percent have flextime options, 48 percent have part-timers, 30 percent have employees who work from home, and 28 percent have job sharing.[3]

"Flexible work arrangements" is the catchall term for part-time, flexible hours, job sharing, temp work, telecommuting, and independent contract work. Each and every flexible work arrangement makes it easier for us to achieve balance between family and work, school and work, and even leisure and work.

As more and more corporations are coming out of the family-unfriendly dark ages, some have been brave enough to put their flexible work guidelines in print. When worldwide consulting firm Deloitte and Touche saw competent women leaving its jobs at the rate of 30 percent annually, it developed the Women's Initiative, a robust series of work-life policies that made its workplace more family-friendly, encouraging women to stay at the firm. Deloitte realized that job turnover translates into expensive and time-consuming retraining. The firm reports some 1,100 professionals on formal flexible arrangements, including eighteen partners on less than full-time schedules.[4] The numbers don't lie. Changes in corporate culture that give women flexibility are happening at Deloitte and dozens of other companies.

The whole idea of part-time employment is as new to many moms as to their employers. When we searched for jobs as single women, how many of us really thought about family-friendly issues or flexibility? But when we go back to work, after being a stay-at-home mom for one year or for a decade, it's crucial to examine company policies as carefully as you sift through the trick-or-treat candy.

Unfortunately, in some instances the company policy supports flexible arrangements, but the pocket cultures buck them. It is not always possible to assess the grassroots support for policies until after you are on the job. "It has to do with the mind-set of the initial recruiter and it has a lot to do with the manager," says Linda Koch, a vice president at Flexible Resources, Inc., a consulting and staffing firm. "A company says they are family-friendly or that they have policies, but do they practice what they preach?" Too often it is not until a company's CEO has a daughter who reenters the workplace or his wife is stricken with a serious illness that the meaning of flextime hits home.

Before you start asking the hard questions of the human resources director, you need to figure out what exactly you want in terms of work: part-time, full-time, job-share, permanent flex hours, flexible flex hours. The choices can be confusing.

FROM THE GOING BACK SURVEY

How did you first return to work?

49 percent: Part-time outside the home
35 percent: Full-time outside the home
13 percent: Part-time at home
 3 percent: Full-time in the home

What Size Are You?

Store shelves are filled with one-size-fits-all T-shirts, but how many women can really wear them? Too tight, too short, wrong neckline. We all know what works best for us. The same is true for jobs. What works for one woman doesn't necessarily work for another. While flexible work arrangements sound good, what are your particular needs? What kind of arrangement do *you* need to fit *your* lifestyle?

Even before you stomp the pavement, flip through the classifieds, or resurrect your Rolodex, you need to prioritize your work-life needs. Get out that agenda book we talked about and make a pie chart. The salary slice—how much money you want to make or need to make—might be the biggest. Thinner slices represent flexible scheduling, vacation time, potential for promotion, the type of work, the office environment, and even the commute. Keep the pie chart handy. As you look into an available position or consider an offer, take a pencil, resection the pie, shade in each slice and see if the particular job looks like it could work for you. For example, you may decide to take less pay in exchange for more vacation time. Or maybe you are willing to take less pay if you can be home before your children return from school. Maybe the job is only part-time but it gets you started on a new career. Maybe the job will not exactly challenge you but there's room for promotion. Remember the soul-searching you did before you started out the door: Do you want a job or a career? What do you want from work in terms of money, satisfaction, challenge? Now you need to answer those questions.

For California hair stylist Marie Ferro, it is important to have a career that she can leave behind when she goes home to her husband and teenage daughter. "I don't have to work when I go home. I'm done. It is not like being a therapist."

Beth O'Connor, an event planner in Green Bay, Wisconsin, is not looking for more projects or clients because her home business is "manageable" and that's the way she likes it. Someday she hopes to specialize in corporate and private parties. For now Beth is willing to trade a bigger paycheck for working at home, saying, "I want to tuck my babies in at night."

When a former high-powered human resources executive with a six-figure salary returned to work, she took a job with a local New England company. Although she made a fraction of her former salary, the new job satisfied her priorities at the time. A mom, living in suburban Connecticut, she knew that the whirlwind corporate world wasn't going to work for her. "Part-time, flexible, and working at home were the operative words," said this mother of two grade school children.

After years at home raising her children and earning an advanced degree, Kathi Morse was anxious to jump into full-time work if she could find an opportunity to make a difference in people's lives. She certainly discovered *that* working as a grief and trauma specialist.

Like each of these moms, you need to assess the various work arrangements out there and decide which works for you. Better yet, create your own. You are not making a lifelong commitment. Contract work or telecommuting might be the best option when your children are in elementary school. Flexible scheduling may be best when they are in middle school. Whichever way you go, remember that in this new world order of flexible work arrangements, it is a win-win situation for you and your employer. Happier employees take less time off and are more productive, more efficient, more committed. In the Ecology of Careers study, Dr. Phyllis Moen found that "success" is not an either-or. "Success at work is not at odds with success at family life. Rather, feeling successful in one domain predicts feeling successful in another."

Part-Time

When someone asks Crisanne Kadamus Blackie, "And what do you do?" she doesn't tell them that she works part-time. With head held high and without missing a beat, she answers that she is a career counselor and coach and a health adviser for the University of Maine. Part-time? It doesn't cross her lips.

Part-timers get a bad rap. You've heard it all: They are not serious about their work; they are working only to keep busy; they are working only to make some extra pocket money. But with almost one-quarter of all female wage earners working part-time, business is finally beginning to wake up and realize that many workers have reprioritized their lives and it has nothing to do with their commitment or competency. We hope that in the near future Crisanne and some six million moms with children under eighteen who work part-time will cry out, "I'm a part-timer and I'm proud." In our online survey, mom after mom either praised part-time work or wished for more part-time opportunities. "I don't think people should be expected to work forty hours a week, but I know that's very idealistic. Someone who works really doesn't have time for family during the week, if you figure it out hour by hour. After work, sleep, commuting, dinner, breakfast, time for self, cleaning, etc., there isn't much time left, if any," wrote Rebecca Miller, of Sammanish, Washington.

Without a doubt, part-time work is the single best way to keep your hand in your career. While the federal government defines part-time as anything less than thirty-five hours a week, for our purposes part-time can be as few as five or ten hours a week. For more than twelve years, Mary taught one course a semester at New York University. She chose a course that the department had a difficult time filling and became a reliable semester-in, semester-out adjunct. She had never intended to work when her children were young, but it quickly became apparent that motherhood did not require her constant presence 24/7. She slowly discovered that most stay-at-home mothers did leave the house! Maybe it was for an exercise class or a trip to the mall. It occurred to Mary that "I go out every week for a few hours and I could either make money or spend money." When she was ready to return to work full-time, she was well positioned to compete for an opening.

Is Part-Time Work for You?
- You can work in a job that you love and still have time for your family and yourself.
- You can ease your way back in slowly, giving you time to make the needed adjustments.
- You can bring your résumé up to date, closing that big gap between your last job and today's date.
- But . . . less money and fewer benefits.
- Less chance for promotion and fewer opportunities to work on challenging projects.

Those stumbling blocks can be overcome if you convince your boss that part-time is synonymous with high-quality work. After six years at home, Laura Steiger started looking for work in a small city about a hundred miles north of Seattle. She saw part-time work as a critical first step in her well-planned strategy to establish a new employment history and get a current reference. With those two items in hand, Laura could apply for a better full-time job when the time was right. The "starter job," as she calls it, was not easy to find, especially in the depressed Northwest economy right after September 11. Laura also wanted more than income and flexibility. Like many women we talked to, Laura also wished for a job where she could "serve the public rather than a big corporation." During her months-long search, she believed some employers rejected her because she had been home for so long. "I was feeling a little mad because society likes to speak about how important it is for a young child to have a full-time parent. Here I am trying to reenter with a big gap. No one wanted to take the chance."

Fortunately, her volunteer work helping to edit and lay out an alternative newspaper paid off. She landed a job as a proofreader and calendar editor at a daily newspaper, the *Bellingham Herald*. The salary is modest and the deadline pressure intense, but it was what she was looking for in terms of a reentry job. Laura's goals for a part-time job are applicable to all returning moms.

- Persuade someone to take a chance on you.
- Reestablish your credibility as a good worker.
- Get a current reference that you can use for your next job.

You must be very clear about what you expect to get out of part-time work, or you may be disappointed. Another crucial question to consider is whether the job can be performed in the time allotted. We heard this complaint over and over when we attended a Flex-Time Lawyers luncheon in New York. Many of the young lawyers were on "supposedly" part-time schedules but were actually putting in full-time hours to get the job done. Sure, it's great to work a three-day-week job, but the amount of work must also be adjusted accordingly. One anonymous reply to our survey from a construction company manager made that very point: "I have a dream situation with work, the flexibility is unlimited. I get paid extremely well. The problem is that there is always something outstanding that needs to be dealt with, and it's kind of a constant stress. I typically work three days a week, seven hours per day, but in a professional environment, this is just not enough to get a thorough job done and be available when people need you. I have a nanny, and once child care is paid, even making a great hourly rate, the nanny and taxes require more than I keep. Although the concept of working three days is enviable and most people think it's the best of all worlds, it's just that in order to work a job that can support child care from part-time wages, the stress is that of a $100,000 job, but you are only getting paid $50,000 for the stress."

So beware of the downsides of part-time but don't be put off by them. Part-time work can be beneficial for both you and your employer. Professors Mary Dean Lee of McGill University and Shelley MacDermid of Purdue University conducted interviews about part-time employees with supervisors, many of whom had inherited these workers. "One of the things that was most striking was that most bosses felt these people were very good workers. There was very little evidence in that report that people working part-time are bad workers," Shelley said. One part-timer exemplified this can-do attitude, telling her, "I work every day like I am going on vacation the next day."

Suellen Mazurowski, the Ohio lawyer, also sings the praises of her two part-time employees, both paralegals, both married women, one of whom is a young mother who works from nine to three. She has found that part-time employees don't waste time. They come in the door ready to hit the ground running and still have energy to spare midafternoon. "I get their best time. When you work four to six hours you are not burned out; you are not totally stressed out."

Part-timers don't use the office hours to make pediatrician appointments or to speak to insurance adjusters about a recent fender-bender. According to Professor MacDermid, some full-time workers report spending a whopping 10 percent of their time on personal chores. Yet, as a manager herself, she sympathizes with others who are hesitant to hire part-timers. The Pentagon often calls Professor MacDermid with a pressing project, so she needs the office staffed five days a week. With a crew of graduate students who work part-time, she admits that it is hard to keep track of their myriad schedules. The solution is wall charts for Monday through Friday, and the grad students themselves are responsible for full-time coverage. "It's up to them to assure that someone is always in the office so I don't have to think about it. Someone is scheduled to be on deck every day."

Part-time is the mother's mantra in the new millennium. For some moms, part-time employment allows them to keep their skills fresh. Still others want to try out a new career by dipping their toes in the water without getting drenched. And some moms need extra cash at Christmas.

For Candace Hill, the holiday season was creeping closer and her gift list was getting longer. Extra expenses—she and her husband had recently purchased a new home in Evanston, Illinois—

left little cash in her checking account. "I could get creative and make chocolate-covered biscotti in the basement or get a job," says Candace, trying to solve this not-so-uncommon cash-crunch dilemma. "But where can I go that I can work at night and weekends, no babysitters to be paid, and get a really good discount on stuff for Christmas?" she asked herself. It didn't take long for her to realize that a part-time job at a local Borders bookstore was the answer.

It had been years since Candace, a former editor, had a paying job outside the home, but she went for her interview at Borders feeling confident and in control. "I am coming to work for you. I can come down on Saturday. What time is good for you?" she said to the manager without taking a breath. Candace says Borders knew they "struck gold" when they learned how much she knew about buying and selling books because of her volunteer experience in her children's elementary school bookstore.

Her immediate objective—getting gifts on a very tight budget—was easily accomplished. When Borders had its fall 40 percent employee-discount day, Candace bought some fifty presents for $300, from books to potted bulbs, from CDs to stationery. The holidays came and went and Candace stayed on at Borders, often joined by her husband and children who hang out, listen to music, and get lots of promotional children's music free and a discount on any book their little hearts desire. "Imagine, I can go to work and easily pick up every single birthday and holiday gift I'm responsible for during my work hours at a thirty-three percent discount. This in itself is worth the job."

It's been four years now, but it's not only the discounts that keep Candace at Borders. She has shaped a position running special events, working three days a week. The horizon is now filled with possibilities she never imagined when she started helping out in the school bookstore. "Creating this schedule depended upon pure luck, staying power, and making myself invaluable at the bookstore," she says. Candace rattles off a laundry list of events that she now spearheads, from the Martin Luther King Day celebration, to story hours, to a Parenting in the 21st Century reading group. This former editor, with a degree in English literature from Northwestern University—she devours Victorian novels—foresees a long-term future at Borders. "I see a career path in this company. I'm hoping when our brand-new store opens next year that I can create a job that is more special events and less shelving."

Candace's strategy for part-time work:

- **Getting the job.** Convinced Borders that her volunteer work at the elementary school bookstore was equivalent to retail.
- **Keeping the job.** Stayed on after the holiday season and took the initiative in expanding her position beyond sales.
- **Enjoying the job.** Draws on her literary background and creativity to organize special events and reading groups.
- **Meshing with her family.** Works same hours as school, and her "bookstore junkie" family visits her on weekends at the store.
- **Earning and saving money.** While her salary is "just tolerable," she compensates by saving on all her gifts thanks to a large discount.

Like Candace, many stay-at-home moms are on a career path without even realizing it. While at home full-time, many moms naturally gravitate toward volunteer positions drawn by the desire to make a difference in some little way. That enthusiasm for a particular cause, whether an arts program for an elementary school or a community fund-raising project or a church soup kitchen, can help showcase talents that lead to a job.

Staci Handschuh's civic activities led to her job, and she wasn't even looking. It came to her! Because of her volunteer work, Staci was well-known in her town, New Milford, New Jersey. She was asked to suggest people to head up a proposed Police Department youth program, which needed someone who could multitask easily, develop programming, win school support, and get community involvement. Realizing that this job would draw on her strengths, Staci replied that *she* would be interested, but only if the position was on flextime. It sounds pretty gutsy for a woman who had been out of the paid workforce for nine years.

But then again, Staci was working but just not getting paid. From serving as president of the Northern New Jersey NOW chapter to launching a Young Women's Forum, Staci had a range of community activities longer than a six-year-old's list for Santa. In 1998, Staci was appointed a commissioner on the Bergen County Commission on the Status of Women. She worked on a project called Court Watch, where she and other volunteers observed judges. Staci had worked with many of the school administrators and was a super-salesperson, having worked sixty-hour weeks in cell phone sales years prior, all of which added up to make her the perfect candidate for the new position. "I did not realize that the volunteer work I was doing would almost seamlessly fit into the exact needs for the job I ultimately landed," says Staci. "I thought that if I went back to work I would work in cooking or catering. I never thought I would be working with kids. I have a passion and I believe I can make a difference."

From Friday night movies to a four-week Red Cross babysitting certification program, the goal of the youth activities is to reduce or eliminate the "hanging out with nothing to do" that often lands kids in trouble. Staci hopes to attract fifteen hundred students, ages twelve to eighteen, into her community programs. One winter night found her at work dressed in ski parka and frolicking in the snow. It was Take Over the Mountain night, at which 150 kids went snow tubing with many of the community police. The night was designed to show students that police are not necessarily "heavies," but can be mentors, teachers, and friends.

The flexible schedule is just one part of Staci's personal pie chart. Job satisfaction and income are two other important slices for her. "I love what I am doing. It feels like I have recharged my life, and I really enjoy the regular paycheck. I almost forgot we can be compensated for our hard work. I had to be called to be reminded to pick up my first check. And I can be working from home in my sweats, drinking coffee. It is much more efficient than in panty hose."

Let's be realistic. Staci was very lucky, although we could also argue that she made her own luck by countless hours of valuable volunteer work. That kind of karma doesn't happen for most of us, so we need to work a little harder to develop a job-hunting strategy. That strategy often requires some revision when things don't go exactly as planned. Sometimes our first instinct is to try to revive our previous career, the work we know and loved, going full-time, full blast. If that doesn't work out, then we need to go to plan B, which often translates to part-time work, perhaps in a completely different field. The idea is not to be discouraged if the first try doesn't work. Take a lesson from the marines: Adapt, improvise, overcome. That's what Linda Koch did when her initial plans to return to her advertising career didn't work out. Linda, an account executive at an international ad agency, went back to work a year after her first child's birth, but the traveling and the job demands were too intense. "The pace of the advertising job was not working with my other needs. I know that I give 110 percent. It was not good for my child or my husband."

So Linda stayed home for eight years, raising a son and a daughter and getting heavily involved with the schools and her community in upstate New York. But when both of her children were in school full days, Linda too decided it was time to go back and soon found herself at a Cos Cob, Connecticut, company called Flexible Resources, which specializes in part-time, job-share, and contract work placement. Linda's initial thought was to try to get back into advertising on a part-time basis. But the jobs she interviewed for never fit right. "The reality is that it doesn't always happen at the moment we think it should. I started to realize that this was going to take some time, so I went ahead and got a brand-new puppy."

She wasn't home long with her new pooch when Flexible Resources called her to work for them. Evidently her personal and administrative skills impressed the agency's executives. "They were drowning and needed some extra hands, and they were willing to train me. I really enjoyed learning a new profession, and I used some of the same people skills I used in advertising."

She started off working during school hours. While the company was very accommodating, Linda says, "I was crazed learning a new business and coming up to speed, but initially I couldn't let go. I had to be there when my kids walked in the door." Linda learned what many women know: The game plan takes tinkering until you get it working smoothly. Again, it might not be the way you first imagined, but if it works, then make the play.

It took only four months for Linda to realize that she couldn't magically divide herself in half and that she was too stressed racing here and there. Eventually, she found a college student who was willing to come three afternoons a week to drive her children to their after-school activities.

On the days that Linda cannot get into the Flexible Resources office, a half-hour drive from her house, she works from home. While she can do certain aspects of her job at home, interviewing is best done in the office. She notes with a laugh, "If I did it from home, the dog would be jumping on the candidates I interview."

Linda's dream may have been to go back into advertising but, at least for now, that was not to be, and that's not a bad thing! "I may always love advertising, but this fits better with my life and the time I have to devote to it. I have more flexibility than most other situations," she says.

Imagine walking into Flexible Resources's office looking for a job and meeting Linda, a woman who understands your mind-set. Some 25 to 30 percent of Linda's clients are mothers just like herself, women who are trying to make the transition back to work. She gets it. She understands a mom's internal tug-of-war. "When I can find a job for a person and give her the balance I have, I really feel good about it. I believe in it. I live it. I practice it."

From Candace's bookstore event planning to Staci's youth programming to Linda's position as a recruiter, part-time work comes in myriad shapes and forms. So toss out that preconceived notion that the job you want can't-won't-couldn't-shouldn't. Instead, let these women inspire you to spin your variation on a theme.

Temp Agencies

Suppose you are truly stumped and have reworked that pie chart so many times that it looks like mush. It's been so long since you looked for a job that both the landscape and lingo have changed. You're not sure whether your child-care arrangements will work out or your three children are in three different schools and descending into car pool hell. One way to get back in slowly and perhaps learn some new skills at the same time is to sign up with a temp agency.

Think temp agency and the immediate image is a twentysomething with a *Married to the Mob* hairdo, smacking gum, filing her nails at the receptionist's desk. Not anymore. Temp agencies have gone the way of the diaper pail; staffing agencies have taken their place. Rather than filling jobs for sick or vacationing employees, staffing agencies fill full-time, temporary positions from clerks to CEOs, from office managers to marketing specialists. Want to return to the cockpit? There are all kinds of boutique staffing firms that specialize in placing corporate pilots.

Why are staffing agencies so popular? First and foremost, they provide a matching service. The good ones understand the culture of the companies they service, making it easier to find a good fit between employee and employer. By signing on with a staffing firm, the older returnee can circumvent possible gray-hair grudges. Sure, age discrimination is illegal, but we all know it's still there. The agency makes the match and conducts the interview and you get in the door to show your stuff. In fact, you are actually hired by the staffing agency as its employee, not by the place you work at day to day.

"'Staffing firm' is simply the term that has become more widely used than 'temp agency,'" says Steven Berchem, vice president of the American Staffing Association. "We actually changed our name in 1999 to better reflect what our members do. It is no longer just staffing but includes permanent placement, training, and human resources consulting."

Not unlike major corporations, staffing agencies attract clients by making the employment packages and perks very attractive. For some, it is the health benefits offered by staffing agencies that go to the top of the list. Others become interested in working for a staffing company when they learn that in addition to health insurance, many agencies offer prescription drug coverage, vision and dental insurance, a 401(k) plan, and sick time pay. And how many people know that vacation plans are available to staffing agency employees, some after ninety days and others as early as the first day of employment?

Training programs are often the big draw. From desktop computer classes to writing résumés, you can learn new skills for free. And if that isn't enough of an incentive, at a staffing firm you can try before you buy. "One of the fastest-growing areas in the staffing industry is so-called temp-to-perm. It lets employees try different environments and see what's best for them," says Mr. Berchem. If you are considering a new field or want to see if your old career still feels comfortable, getting a temporary job through a staffing firm allows you to work for a designated period of time before making the final commitment. Do you want to work in a small office or a large corporation? How do you feel about commuting? Is early in/early out the best schedule for you? You can try out one of the many flexible work arrangements on a temporary basis before deciding what fits the bill.

Staffing agencies even work effectively with hard-to-place moms like military spouses who get transferred along with their husbands every few years. Happy wives make happy sailors, so the navy is trying to make it easier for spouses of servicemen and -women to find jobs or build careers. The Department of the Navy, looking to increase retention in the service, joined with Adecco, the world's largest staffing agency, to provide career counseling, training, and job placement for navy and marine spouses at no cost to either the spouses or to the military.

When the marines transferred Bernadette Dallam's husband to Kaneohe Military Base in Kailua, Hawaii, she was ready and raring to start a new career. Bernadette, the mother of two young children, had recently received an associate degree in business from the Technical College of the Low Country in South Carolina where her husband had been stationed. To Bernadette's surprise and great disappointment, finding a job was not as easy as she thought it would be. Some prospective employers questioned how long she would be stationed in Hawaii. Discouraged but determined, Bernadette attended a job fair on the base where she learned about Adecco's partnership with the military and liked what she heard. "I can move from one base to the next and still hold my benefits. It is awesome. If I go to another state, town, or country, it makes it easier for me to be placed. I could not believe it. I was trying hard to hold back tears."

Adecco offered her an assignment as a human resources generalist at the Waikiki Beachcomber Hotel. After a month of looking for a job halfway around the world from her last home, Bernadette landed a great position. "I really didn't believe it. I was almost falling over in my chair."

At the hotel, Bernadette replaced a woman who was on a

FACTS YOU NEVER KNEW ABOUT STAFFING AGENCIES[5]

- 90 percent of staffing companies provide free training for their temporary employees. From computer training to sales, new skills are yours for the asking.
- 2 million people per day are employed by staffing companies.
- 72 percent of employees get permanent jobs within the first year while working for a staffing company.
- 45 percent of temporary employees don't want to change their work arrangement and prefer their work over traditional employment.
- 29 percent of temporary employees go into a permanent position with the company they were assigned.
- Staffing firm employees are protected under the same laws applicable to traditional workers.

three-month maternity leave. "It was the best experience of my life," she says gleefully. Then she took another assignment as a management assistant at Kaiser Permanente's Clinical Information System, transferring written information to computers. "There is no end date, so I play it by ear," she says, sounding confident and relaxed about how her career is now going.

Bernadette made the decision to register with a staffing agency for a number of reasons. First of all, she had felt an unfair bias during her job search. "Some of the locals have a mind-set that you won't be here, and they feel the locals have to be placed first," she says. "Some of the locals will only last for a few weeks. I can guarantee that the three years I am here I will bust my butt." Her job allowed her to test new waters. Bernadette had never worked as an HR generalist. She liked it, she was successful at it, and now she has another job to add to her résumé.

Perhaps the uncertainty of her marine husband's assignments is another reason Bernadette is so happy to find permanent employment. "It is hard for us. We don't know when our husbands are sent away. The program is the best thing that ever happened to me. I love to be home with my children and to work."

Night Shift

Listen up, women: It is time to think out of the box. When it seems like you can't find a way to go back, consider some of these creative solutions. If you want to be home when the children return from school, look into night-shift work. Forty percent of women with children under the age of eighteen work different shifts than their significant others.[6] It is so common that the U.S. Census Bureau has given it a name: tag-team day care.

When Denise Nielson was laid off from her nine-to-five job as a legal secretary in 1998, she did some consulting work for eighteen months. Needing a steady income, she looked for a night-shift position at a law firm, many of which are staffed twenty-four hours a day. She called around to some agencies, and after a three-month trial period to see if she could handle the night shift, she was hired permanently for a thirty-hour week with benefits. "I will tell you that being laid off was the best thing that happened to me," she says.

Denise travels thirty miles south from her home in Lawrenceville, Georgia, to an Atlanta law firm to work as a word processor. Her children are home by the time she leaves for work at five P.M. as her husband walks in the door. "The upside is that I can be here for school activities and be home with my toddler as well. I think a lot of women could profit from understanding the benefits of night shift. The wonderful thing about my schedule is that I had so much guilt when I was working the normal nine-to-five, but I don't have that feeling now. I went back to work kicking and screaming, but once the money came back, it was really a blessing."

Denise sees this night-shift work as a temporary solution. She has a college degree from the University of LaVerne in Southern California and plans to run her own business someday. "For now, the pay is good and it works well for us." If you need a transitional job, if your husband is suddenly out of work, if you are loath to let anyone other than a parent care for your child, think night shift. It might be a good short-term solution.

Job Sharing

Loretta did not know she was a woman ahead of her times. When her youngest was a toddler, she decided that she wanted some part-time work. She was looking for a job, not a career, but little did she know that the job would last some eighteen years.

When a neighbor suggested that she work at his travel agency as a consultant, she jumped at the opportunity. She is the first to admit that the actual job was not the draw as much as the lure of New York City, some thirty miles from her suburban home, twice a week. She loved being an at-home mom but longed for adult stimulation and something to call her own. It did not take long for her to realize that being in the office just two days was not enough for her clients. It was then that she asked her good friend and neighbor, Janet Boxer, to job-share.

Between Loretta and Janet, the office was covered Monday through Thursday, and they were both available by phone on Fridays. They worked side by side on Mondays and Thursdays and each worked solo one day a week. What made the arrangement unique and comfortable for both Loretta and Janet was that they also babysat for each other's small children on the days they did not work. When Janet was in the office alone, Loretta covered the home front, and vice versa. Their children were in the same grades and their little boys were best friends—and still are. Needless to say, the kids loved the arrangement as much as their moms did. On the days that Loretta and Janet worked together, they shared a babysitter, which also pleased everyone.

This was a tag team in the truest sense of the word. In the office, their desks were side by side, making it easy to hear each other on the phone, pass files back and forth, or share a bagel. "Together we make one perfect person," Loretta frequently said. "We could hear each other speaking to the clients and kept current on all the bookings, no matter who made the reservations. We would update each other every evening so we both knew what had transpired in the other's absence. When a client called, more often than not he or she would ask, 'Is this Loretta or Janet?' It honestly did not matter who the client was speaking to because both of us were totally familiar with all the bookings, reservations, and trip plans in progress."

Job sharing is not new. It started in the '70s when secretarial responsibilities were split between two people. Today, it is definitely on the upswing. Twenty-eight percent of companies offer job sharing, up from 18 percent in 1990.[7]

Shari Rosen Ascher knows firsthand about job sharing. She and Maggie Sisco both worked selling national radio time in New York City. Maggie left when her first child was born, and Shari followed soon after. At the time, they contemplated job sharing, but their idea was not well received by their previous employer so they brought their idea to a competitor, Interep Radio, which was willing to give them a try. As TeamShaggie, they rose from account executive to vice president of sales, each working three days a week, overlapping on Wednesday.

In 2000, they started their own new business, ShareGoals, a consulting firm for both individuals and companies that want to jump on the job-sharing bandwagon. The company advised would-be job sharers and companies interested in learning to manage job-share teams. They also self-published a book, *Share the Goals—How to Successfully Job Share.* From counseling on job sharing to running seminars on writing job-sharing policies for major corporations like Vivendi, Viacom, and Lever Brothers, these women quickly got face and name recognition, appearing on national TV and in magazines. They hired a public relations person, and these super-saleswomen even had lip balm made that said "most consultants only give lip service."

Unfortunately, after 9/11, the company suffered setbacks and had to make some difficult choices. During 2002, after being involved in community and school-based organizations, Shari promised herself that she would return only to work that was fulfilling to her. In addition to running their Web site, www.share-goals.com, giving interviews, and selling their books, Shari has taken a job in underwriting and development at WFUV, a non-profit radio station at Fordham University. Because Maggie provided the health benefits for her family, she returned to work at

Interep as a VP of sales with a new job-share partner, who was brought to her by their manager.

"We were forced to separate, but we didn't want to divorce," explains Shari, who job-shared with Maggie for almost eight years. "I love job sharing because having a partner gives you an incredible support system. No one really gets it unless she has done it. It's an incredible way to return. You have someone with you and it is not as scary. It made my life so much easier and so complete."

Can we all be job sharers? Definitely not. If you are the kind of woman who likes to fly solo, forget about job sharing. And if you are not a good communicator, job sharing is not for you. Shari says that it is important to fill each other in on everything that goes on, even a mundane joke a client told at a meeting. You and your partner must be on the same wavelength. You have to be able to complete each other's sentences, know what the other is thinking. It helps if you have the same values about work life and family life. You can't be small-minded or petty. The workload split might not always look equal, but you must believe that in the end it will be. If your job-sharing partner's three kids get the flu, you have to cover. You have no choice. The tables will be turned when you have to make an unexpected trip to care for an ailing parent in another state.

We like to say that we job-share, writing magazine articles and books together for more than eight years. People are amazed to hear we have never had an argument. Maybe that's because we are rarely in the same room! Seriously, it works on several levels. First, and most important, we both love the collaboration of bouncing ideas back and forth, talking about interviews, and passing copy between us electronically. While we often amaze ourselves at how we think alike, we also bring different perspectives to our work and believe that makes for a better book. Finally, neither is keeping a checklist tracking who is doing more. In writing this book, for example, Loretta did the heavy lifting during the spring season when Mary had a difficult teaching load and while her son, a marine lieutenant, was in Iraq. And during the push in the summer, while Loretta was planning a wedding for her daughter, Mary carried more of the workload. So it can work wonderfully; it's just a matter of finding the right partner.

Another variation on job sharing allows partners to be in different locations. Do you know the perfect partner to team up with but she lives on the opposite coast? Consider bicoastal job sharing. If you are on the West Coast, you start your work three hours later than your East Coast partner.

Be prepared to be turned down. Not all companies are open to job sharing. You will get a warmer welcome if you have a proven track record as a partner on a team. It's even better if both you and your partner look for a job together and have proof of past successes. But there are dinosaurs out there. If you are proposing a job-share arrangement to someone who hasn't worked with job-share teams and doesn't know how terrific your team is, no matter how convincing your case is, you may be turned down.

Talk about being ahead of their time, two other job sharers not only partner seamlessly, they also run a placement agency that specializes in flexible work arrangements from job sharing to telecommuting to contract or part-time positions. The aptly named Flexible Resources was cofounded in Greenwich, Connecticut, fourteen years ago by baby boomers Laurie Young and Nadine Mockler, who realized that while moms cherished motherhood, they also wanted to work, but not nine to five, Monday through Friday. "With globalization and technology, the full-time work schedule is outdated," says Laurie, with the same conviction of a mother who tells her disbelieving toddler, "Broccoli is good for you."

Laurie and Nadine, armed with MBAs, bring the same dedication, passion, and commitment to their clients and their company. They coordinate their schedules, with one of them always in the office. They even planned their second pregnancies in tandem so that they would not be expecting their babies at the same time.

Speaking from experience, both Laurie and Nadine, mothers of three children each, practice what they preach. Flexible Resources has ten employees in four offices and they are all moms and all work part-time. Laurie explains, "The company was started as a mommy-track company. Now we provide access to a group of talent that some companies weren't looking at."

From Pitney Bowes to Playtex, from Lipton to Liz Claiborne, their client list reads like the who's who of American business. "I work with businesses to make them recognize the benefits of these professional women," says Laurie. "Many are capable moms who have not been in business but have run the PTO. They are bright, articulate, organized, mature women whom I would pay to be in my customer service department."

Laurie has some solid advice for moms returning to the workforce: "Don't be apologetic. At an interview, tell them, 'Here is what I have to offer.'" And in case we didn't hear it the first time,

Laurie repeats, "Don't apologize for not working." She believes that those years at home honed many skills that are transferable to the paid workforce.

Specifically, she recommends middle-management positions as a good match for returnees. "Their egos are not involved and they are not looking for a stepping-stone. It is a place where you can build confidence without the politics."

JOB-SHARING TIPS

- Find a name for the team. Shari and Maggie call themselves "TeamShaggie," which is the name on their business cards and on their office door.
- Answer the phone with the team name. In fact, both women should have the same phone number. "The nickname is about streaming communication with everyone that has to talk to you," explains Maggie.
- If you are not the groundbreaking type, consider industries where job sharing already exists. Pharmaceutical companies, for example, tend to employ large numbers of women for sales and offer more job sharing.
- Look for a partner who has complementary strengths. In other words, don't look for a partner who is your mirror image. If one of you has a strong business sense while the other is a better writer, you are each bringing valuable assets to the table.
- Forget the pronoun "I". It's now "we" on telephone messages, in correspondence, and in casual conversations. You are branding yourself as a successful professional partnership.

Part-Time Lawyers? Stop Pulling My Leg

Who would think that women lawyers need a support group? Everyone knows that these überprofessionals are strong enough to carry a thick *Black's Law Dictionary* in one hand, an overstuffed briefcase in the other, and the weight of an impending verdict on their shoulders. Their feathers don't ruffle when a seasoned six-footer with a gavel sternly says, "Counselor, approach the bench." Yet when it comes to asking the firm for a reduced work schedule to spend more time with their kids, these well-educated whipper-snappers need help. Some might think that it's impossible to be a part-time lawyer.

But not Deborah Epstein Henry. When Deborah's husband took a job in Philadelphia, she was already pregnant with their second son, so she decided to look for a part-time job. Schnader Harrison Segal & Lewis LLP, a large Philadelphia-based law firm, agreed to take her on with a three-quarters schedule and salary. Her new family-friendly work schedule allowed her to stay home on Wednesdays and Fridays, except for an occasional client meeting, court appearance, or deposition. Deborah theorizes why the firm accepted her on her own terms: "I benefited from a hot lateral market and with the presumption I was a well-trained New York lawyer."

However, she craved the comforting ear of other lawyers who were in similar situations. "I felt very isolated and had informal lunches with three other women who were Schnader part-time litigators. We talked about the issues and the good and bad things about being part-timers. Even my Yale roommates, part-time doctors, were struggling." So Deborah sent out six e-mails to other part-time lawyers in Philadelphia, inviting them to a brown bag lunch and suggesting they bring colleagues who wanted to discuss the issues. Those six e-mails brought together eighteen women in July 1999, who ate sandwiches while hashing out their personal employment dilemmas. The Philadelphia mailing list has swelled to more than 350, including two male part-timers.

The Philadelphia organization has been so successful that Deborah has taken her idea to New York City. Coming together one winter day in a swank conference room at a Wall Street law firm, sixty-four women—some with babies at home and others with babies on the way—shared similar fears about being part-timers. "Will I be thrown off the partner track?" "Will I be getting three-quarters salary but still putting in a full-timer's hours?" "Should I forget about doing litigation work?"

Armed with Diet Snapples and brown bag lunches, these women gathered to hear Professor Joan Williams, director of Worklife Law at American University's Washington College of Law, address their apprehensions and answer their questions. She warned of "schedule creep," when an attorney has a reduced schedule but cycles up to full-time, without the appropriate pay. Applauding the work of Flex-Time Lawyers, Professor Williams told the women, "Law has to change. It takes a leap of imagination."

Both Joan Williams and Deborah Epstein Henry refuse to believe that there is any practice area in the legal profession that is not suitable for part-timers. "Every single job can be restructured as part-time," says Deborah. "Litigation is not an easy career and I am not naïve about that, but there are creative solutions."

A burning issue for part-time lawyers is whether the upward career track toward partnership is out of the question. "I had my pick when I came to Philadelphia. I had seven offers. I would not be at a place that wouldn't advance me," Deborah says. But she does admit that part-time partnership is still an uphill battle at many law firms, and the timing for part-timers climbing the ladder may be slightly different. "Often a partnership is delayed until you meet the requisite number of hours, or you are up for partner after you net the number of hours of a full-time associate."

Professor Williams jolts the group by noting, "Unlike business-women, who are rated high in competence, housewives are rated as low in competence, alongside the elderly, the blind, the 're-tarded' and disabled—and working mothers are rated closer to housewives than to businesswomen." She concludes the New York City meeting with words of encouragement: "Start sharing infor-mation. This is a structural problem. Don't be depressed. We are making progress."

DOS AND DON'TS OF A FLEXIBLE ARRANGEMENT

- Do not be afraid to negotiate a deal. If you don't ask, it can never happen.
- Don't expect to have an open-ended arrangement. More often than not, a manager will green-light your work schedule but tell you it's for a designated period of time. Remember, you may be breaking new ground, so tread softly.
- Don't expect all your fellow workers to be thrilled with your arrangement. They are nervous that your flextime might trans-late into overtime for them.
- Don't think that flextime means less time. It is often the same amount of time but in different places.

- Don't take a job without learning as much as possible about your boss. Managers in cubicles do not always happily carry out guidelines coming down from corporate suites.
- Don't undervalue yourself. Just because it has been years since you received a paycheck, your worth as a paid employee does not decrease. Put a dollar value on the experience you gained from chairing committees, leading community action groups, working in the schools, as well as knowledge gained from your work years.
- Don't be inflexible. "Flexible" is a two-way street. Sometimes as an employee you have to be willing to adjust the flexible arrangement or pitch in with extra hours when things get crazy.
- If you take these don'ts to heart, you will know what you should *do*. Do unto others . . . you know the rest.

Finding Full-Time Work That Works

The back-to-work stories of two women we met, both named Mary, one East Coast, the other West Coast, are templates for how to get and keep a good full-time job and not lose your mind, at least most of the time. Their experiences prove the maxims of going back:

- A progressive transition works best in terms of career as well as family.
- Sometimes you have to start at a job that is "beneath" you in terms of skills.
- You have to readjust your time commitment to work over the years.

- Living close to where you work can make a tremendous difference in the stress level.
- You have to loosen the reins on the household, and sometimes the to-do list may not all get done.
- If you ask for flexibility—and prove your worth to a company—you can get it.
- Even if you are out for five years or more, you can snare a great job that challenges you and offers emotional and economic rewards.

The reality of being out for fourteen years often means starting over. Mary Baskauskas of Palo Alto, California, knew that. She also knew that she did not want to recharge her career as an office products marketing representative. Nearby Stanford University seemed like an ideal place to work in terms of both opportunities and location, and with four children under fourteen, she wanted to start slowly. Mary admits with a laugh that she "gravitated toward all the moms who worked at Stanford at her children's elementary school." Finally, one mom mentioned that there was an opening for a part-time administrative assistant in the law school's alumni office. "The mom told me, 'The job is probably beneath you as a basic assistant job,' but I just wanted to learn the law school. I wasn't too concerned about the money. I was much more concerned about not getting in over my head. The position offered great benefits and great training." The great hours, from ten to two, as well as the opportunity to take computer courses sealed the deal.

Two years later, Mary was offered a full-time position in the law school's development office. Not ready to make that transition yet, she interviewed and counteroffered three-fourths time, from nine to three. Her previous experience and performance got her the flex position. For the next three years she learned about development and fund-raising. It was in some ways very similar to her BC career as a sales rep; this was just a "softer sell." Her step up to full-time came three years later when she was encouraged to apply for assistant director of development. "I got it without a search, which was extremely validating. Everyone knew me, my work ethic, knew I had the background, and that I knew the law school." Mary's current position is quite a change from her first job. She puts in ten-hour days and travels a few days each month to meet law school alumni including Hollywood producers, authors, Supreme Court justices, and politicians. For Mary and many other women, the progression from part-time to full-time works both in terms of flexibility when the children are younger and then feeding their career ambitions in later years.

The demanding schedule has changed her family's lifestyle. Her daughters were nineteen and seventeen and her sons were fifteen and twelve when Mary went back full-time. She finds it difficult to manage the household as she did before, even with her husband's added help. But things do work out: She waited too late to sign up her son for summer camp so he's started a vacation pet care service instead. "The kids will complain about little things like the fact that I rarely make cookies anymore. Well, we can buy them. Before going back to work I was the kids' mom and my husband's wife but wasn't doing a lot for me. Now I have more of my own identity."

One summer day we met Mary on the sixty-fifth floor of the Chrysler Building in New York City during a business trip. As we sat in a conference room overlooking Manhattan, Mary looked confident in a green silk suit, as if she had been wheeling and dealing with movers and shakers for years. She had just convinced an international lawyer to chair his law school class's alumni reunion and fund-raising drive. She reflected on the changes over the last five years. "At first I thought maybe I was too old to start a new career; maybe I was being too ambitious. Then as I went along, I realized there was no reason not to set new goals. I have no less to offer now than when I was thirty-five and, in many ways, I have more, with maturity, wisdom, and a lot of different life experiences."

As we rode down in the elevator, the conversation turned to more mundane domestic matters and Mary laughed about what was going on at home in California where her husband was in charge. "The house is a disaster, I am sure. But just as long as they straighten up before I get home, that's okay!"

The East Coast Mary exemplifies another variation on finding work that works. When we talked to Mary Burich, she was just back from a business trip to Napa Valley, where she had a "summit meeting" with the executive chefs employed by Delaware North Companies, Inc., a $1.6-billion corporation. Headquartered in Buffalo, the company manages hospitality services at airports, sporting venues, parks, and resorts, and has a gaming interest as well.

How did this mother of three children—then ages one, five, and eight—jump-start her career after being at home for five years? She used the strategies we suggested earlier: networking, pinpointing what was most important, setting her sights on a realistic goal, and a willingness to be flexible.

Through the birth of her second child, Mary worked as a public relations manager at Fisher-Price in northwestern New York

State. While at home she did some freelance projects and kept up her work contacts, one of whom told her about the opening at Delaware North Companies. She clearly remembers the day the call came from her former boss, now at Delaware North. "The baby was crying and the laundry was going. I was overwhelmed and didn't know how I could ever work. I told her the position would have to be part-time because I have a one-year old and another in preschool and another in grade school. I felt that I was all over the map."

Yet Mary was intrigued by the job offer and knew that she could handle the work. "My marketing technique was to offer more experience than the company was possibly planning on getting in exchange for some flexibility in terms of schedule." Mary had assumed she would stay home about ten years, and when she didn't hear anything about the position for a few months, she thought it was all for the best. Then she got a call offering her the job with part-time hours, including two days working from home. "The position can grow as your kids get older," she was told.

Her strategy worked because she offered a good résumé, even if it was five years old, and because she was very clear about her terms. "I tell other moms to pick what's most important and let that be your point of negotiation. You can't have everything; for me it was hours. I really held to my guns that I had to be part-time. I said, 'I don't care what title you give me, but you have to cut me slack.'"

Over a period of three years, the job morphed into more hours. "I have a hard time saying no," says Mary, laughing. "When you have a flexible arrangement that works, you do try to do your best for the company. I still retain flexibility. I tell them in terms of work that it will get done. It may not get done in conventional hours. I may be doing e-mail at midnight or five A.M., but I will manage."

Mary and the many other mothers we talked to prove our point. If companies are willing to bend and change the way they think about the structure of work, they stand to gain much in return. "I don't know why more companies don't offer flexibility," says Mary. "They get so much back from associates who have balance. We will do whatever we need to do to keep those arrangements because we know how rare and special they are. You get a lot more commitment when you give people that latitude, and with technology there is no reason not to. It works."

Against the Odds

Timing is everything. Diana O'Brien left her job as a consultant at Deloitte and Touche's Cincinnati office in 1992, just one year before the firm inaugurated the Women's Initiative, a program offering a variety of flexible work arrangements. Like so many women we met, Diana's traveling was getting to be too taxing, so she decided to look for another position. For the next three years, Diana worked as director of retail operations at a job with the promise of less travel. During that time Diana found out she was pregnant with triplets. She took a leave, and when her children were born, she opted for a severance package when the company was sold and the headquarters were moved to New York.

Like so many moms, Diana searched for a part-time position but couldn't find one. Finally, she decided to consider a full-time offer at a company that was known to be family-friendly and promised flexibility. Skeptical, but hopeful, she brought the proposal to a mentor at Deloitte, looking for an honest appraisal of the offer. To her surprise, Deloitte countered by saying that they could do better.

During her three-year absence, Deloitte got its Women's Initiative up and running. In an effort to retain competent employees, Deloitte's Women's Initiative offered to women—and men—flexible and alternative work arrangements. "My job was flexible and I had the opportunity to change it every year," explains Diana. "The first year I worked three days a week, the second year I worked four days, and the third year I took an extended leave."

It may come as a surprise that Diana's flexible work scheduling did not thwart her upward career path and she became a partner. But when the triplets were three, they were diagnosed with autism, and once again everything had to change. Diana and her husband both took leaves from their jobs and spent eight weeks in Boston at a school to help teach them and their children how to deal with autism. "The firm has been very supportive of my flexible work arrangement, and they were incredible when my kids were diagnosed," says Diana.

Helping the triplets with their communication and sensory problems, the O'Briens now have a team of fifteen therapists and a doctor who come to their home. The triplets go to school in the home's converted basement as well as to a special education class in a neighborhood school. Diana's husband has become a full-time at-home dad, supervising the activities of his two daughters and son, who require untold attention. When not with the triplets, David, who worked in health care and fund-raising, devotes his time to raising money for autism. Diana is back working full-time, with a curtailed travel schedule. "Deloitte raised the bar for all professional service firms when they began focusing on women. I have a great deal of control over my work, my schedule, and my time. I have the flexibility to do what I need to do when I need to do it: I can work from home when I need to, I do e-mail at night, I may work on the weekends. I believe this is a great place for both men and women; we have opportunity and flexibility to thrive both personally and professionally."

LEARN THE LINGO

Flextime. Introduced in Germany in the early 1960s as a way to solve transit and traffic congestion, this is the most popular work option today. Although flextime is often full-time, think of it as your own personalized work schedule. The two most popular kinds of flextime are traditional and daily. Traditional flextime allows you to begin and end work at the time you choose but may include certain core hours that the employer determines. Daily flextime allows employees to vary the start and stop hours on a daily basis. About one-third of full-time workers have schedules that allow them to vary the time they begin or end their day.[8]

Part-Time. If you work fewer than thirty-five hours a week, you are a part-timer. This may be the employee's choice or the employer's choice. If you are lucky, you can choose the hours and the days that best accommodate home and work needs.[9]

Independent contractor. Sometimes referred to as a freelancer, or an independent consultant, an independent contractor can be self-employed or salaried by the employer. This work can be both entrepreneurial and project oriented.

Job sharing. The work arrangement where two people share one job as a team. Generally, the team splits the workweek. Together, their job would be considered one full-time position. If the place of employment offers benefits to part-timers, then each member of the team qualifies for benefits.

Telecommuting. Perfect for those who prefer pajamas to panty hose. You can work outside the office setting, in your home or a satellite office.

On-Call Worker. From substitute teachers to nurses, this is a great choice for those who like to live spontaneously and are willing to stay close to an answering machine or cell phone. It is not great for those who need to know their schedules in advance for child care.

Contract Work. Usually an older person (the median age is forty, and one out of five contract workers is over fifty) whose employment is contractual for a particular service, often for a given period of time.[10] From lawyers to scientists to IT specialists, this is a good way to go in and out of the workforce.

Agency temp. In this case, the employer is the temp or staffing agency, which can provide both long-term and short-term gigs. Signing on with a staffing agency is a good way of trying something new.

Girl Ghettos

Some women want nothing less than a full-time job with commensurate salary and benefits. But they don't want to negotiate flexibility; they want it part and parcel of the position. Are there full-time jobs with built-in flexibility? Sure there are, but guess what? They're the very ones you turned your nose up at years before.

We call them girl ghettos, jobs that are predominately female. More than 82 percent of elementary school teachers, 93 percent of nurses, and a whopping 97 percent of the secretaries, typographers, and typists are female. And almost 62 percent of psychologists are women.[11] So don't rule out those traditionally female careers, because many work well for returning moms.

All of these girl ghettos offer interesting flexibility. Mulling over the possibilities for a second career, many moms are attracted to teaching, for example, because of the hours and vacation time. What many are surprised to find, when they take the plunge into education classes and student teaching, is that they actually love the challenge and rewards of shaping young minds. Yet they never considered teaching right out of college because it was "women's work."

TEACHING

Many women start back with jobs as a teacher's aide. For some that is where they begin and end. Others find that a door opens to a career they never expected. In Anchorage, Alaska, former navy medic Laurie Rodgers started working as a teacher's aide because she didn't know exactly what else to do. When a sixth grader faced not graduating, Laurie tutored her in math for an entire day while the rest of the class was on a field trip. A month later, the student arrived at the sixth-grade graduation in tears and told her that she never would have graduated if Laurie had not taught her another way to look at math. "That was it! I was hooked. I was a teacher," says this mother of three children. Once she had the epiphany, it almost seemed obvious. "I was hanging around the school anyway," she says.

When Susan Seigel was a young woman going off to college, her mother urged her to take some education courses. Like many moms in the '70s, Sue's mom thought that teaching was the panacea. Summer vacations, school holidays, good hours. And, "You can always go back." But like many other American daughters at the time, Susan told her mom, "I don't have to be a teacher just because I am a girl."

It was the sciences that were a magnet for Susan, and instead of becoming a teacher, she became a supervisor in a microbiology research laboratory. After marrying and having a child, she decided to be a full-time mom. Fast-forward fifteen years and we find Susan in Freehold High School teaching science to a group of incredibly motivated seniors. When her youngest was ten years old, Sue decided to return to school to take education courses with the hopes of becoming a teacher. But why the change of heart? During her at-home years she had worked in her children's school on planning committees, and she loved being there. She came to believe that being a teacher "would be a perfect world."

Susan has been back for some seven years now, teaching a medical science program in a school just ten minutes from her home. It's a biochemistry research class in which the kids do their own impressive projects. She also teaches sophomore biology. "I turn kids on to science," says Susan. "You would think it would be different now, but the girls are still not into it." Going back has taken another twist and turn for Susan. She has been asked by a local college to instruct science teachers who will be teaching a medical sciences program in high schools.

NURSING

Nursing used to evoke images of starched white uniforms and Florence Nightingale capes. No longer. Today nurses wear everything from pants to animal print shirts to street clothes covered with keep-me-clean painters' smocks. And if your vision of a nurse is a woman walking down a hospital corridor balancing a medication tray with one hand and rolling a blood pressure machine with the other, think again. Nurses are now working on insurance company hot lines, in corporate headquarters, and in schools.

A registered nurse with twenty years of experience, Lisa Graziano has a job that is so neomillennium that this forty-year-old mother of two doesn't even see her patients. After answering an advertisement in the *Buffalo News*, Lisa took a job as a telephone triage nurse, working the midnight-to–eight A.M. shift. Fielding as many as forty calls on a busy night, Lisa is the professional intermediary between the physician and the patient.

Although Lisa works in western New York State, her call center represents fifty to sixty practices, some as far south as New York City. From pediatrics to geriatrics, her cases range from rashes to high fevers. When she gives advice as a telephone triage nurse she follows physician-approved guidelines. "In the initial assessment, we do demographics, including the patient history, to help present the case to the physician over the phone. The callers have the option to speak to the doctor, but a lot are afraid to wake the doctor up. We page the physician, and she calls back."

"What can this rash be?" one frantic parent asks Lisa. "Does this cough sound serious?" asks another. "We have had instances where we have to call 911," says Lisa. Having children of her own, Lisa sympathizes with the concern she hears in the voices of moms and dads who call the center. "Even being a nurse, I was a nervous wreck with my first daughter," she says. "We calm them down."

Sometimes the caller realizes the seriousness of the situation but is hesitant to go straight to the hospital because of insurance company red tape. "The person calling in says, 'My insurance company says I have to call the doctor first.'"

After hearing about Lisa's telephone nursing, we had to ask the obvious question: Can Lisa find job satisfaction as a nurse without the human contact? "I actually find it wonderful," she says. "I am doing a lot of patient education. Parents are looking for help to get through the night and need more information."

Working at the center two to three nights each week, Lisa finds time to continue her work as a day care center consultant, monitoring the safety and health of children. New York State mandates that all day care centers have a consultant on staff. Lisa works for six family-run day care centers near Lake Erie, not far from her home in Buffalo. Making the rounds of the six centers once every three or four months, Lisa instructs the centers about administering medication and assessing a sick child's health problems. She is also available as a go-between when management and parents are at odds.

So maybe Lisa's father wasn't wrong when he told his young daughter that nursing is an excellent profession, that she could always support herself, that she could always work. "Nursing is a great job," says Lisa. "Very few of my friends and relatives can say they have the best of both worlds. I can work around anything in my life. We don't always get the best pay or benefits, and maybe it's not a very prestigious position, but I can work around my husband, I can have my child full-time, and have my career. And being in a female-dominated field, it is not uncommon for employees to become pregnant and leave. Lots of nurses are mothers, married, and employers tend to be more understanding. There are always patients and always a need for nurses."

Registered nurse Cindy Sofia, from Manalapan, New Jersey, doesn't see patients either. Like Lisa, she too is using the intensive training she received as a registered nurse. Cindy, now incorporated as Sofia Associates, LLC, checks the credentials of physicians who want to become part of the insurance company she represents. Covering the entire state of New Jersey and parts of New York, Cindy started on her own but now has a team of eight to ten women working for her. "Most of the women are my friends," says Cindy. She had tried some full-time, per diem work after having children, but found that she came home drained both mentally and physically.

Time and time again, work comes our way from parents at a PTA meeting, on the soccer field, and even through relatives. In Cindy's case it was her husband who worked for the insurance company that needed a nurse to do site visits. "I can do this while the children are in school. I am home when they get home, and a lot of the people I hire have the same situation. It's great for moms who want to return. It's a good job for extra money."

Originally the insurance company wanted everyone on her team to be a nurse, but now as long as they have some medical knowledge they can join Cindy's group. "I train everyone and go on the first site visits."

On a busy week, Cindy will make somewhere between ten to fifteen visits to doctors' offices. "There is just so much shopping you can do," she says jokingly. "It kind of makes you feel useful, doing something else other than car pooling. It allows me flexibility; I meet lots of people; I don't need to be in a hospital."

Crisscrossing the state, Cindy marches into a physician's office armed with a four-page checklist. The first three pages ask about the doctor's hospital affiliations, staffing, and scheduling, as well as some basic office safety issues such as access to fire extinguishers. Walking through the site—sometimes with the doctor and often with the office manager—she works her way down the list, making notations. Her training as a nurse comes into play when she examines patients' charts, making sure that the doctors made important notations like patients' allergies and laboratory results.

Cindy is the first to admit that the actual office visits are not difficult. In fact, the scheduling is often more challenging than the inspections. You could say that Cindy is now in management. She personally reviews all the work of the women on her team. If the women in the field have any issues with the doctors they visit, they know to call her immediately. Happily, her business runs smoothly as long as she has responsible people doing the visits. Unfortunately, she says, some women sign on and then don't show up for the visits. When that happens she jumps in and does the work herself. "That is why I prefer to get people that I know or someone recommended," she says.

For Cindy, the part-time job has evolved into a responsible position. "I never thought it would come to where it has, that I can take charge and have my own territory. I never thought this little venture would turn into this much. It's nice to look back and say, 'Look what I did.'" Jokingly, she adds, "And I have learned to read a map very well."

FLIGHT ATTENDANT

The movie *Catch Me if You Can* portrayed 1960s stewardesses (aka "stews") as glamour queens strutting down the airport walkways in color-coordinated designer outfits, right down to their hats, gloves, and purses. Forty years later finds many flight attendants dressed in navy-blue-so-it-won't-show-the-stains uniforms, cleaning out the seat-back pockets before passengers board after a thirty-minute layover. The glamour went out the window with deregulation. Still, many flight attendants love their jobs and return to them after being at home because of both the built-in flexibility and job satisfaction. In Dallas, Liz and Pete Campbell are a flight attendant–pilot couple who stagger their workdays, allowing one parent always to be at home. Liz works on international flights, usually flying five trips each month.

"For me being a flight attendant and a mom is the perfect combination. I can trade a trip if I have to be home for a soccer game. I make switches every month," says Liz. "I drop at least one trip or maybe two. I work around fifty hours a month; I could work up until 120 hours a month, hard-core flight hours from engines on to engines off. (When I show up one hour early to set up or for briefing, I am not getting paid.) I am gone for three days, home five, and then gone again."

Liz doesn't always run around sightseeing the minute she hits some fascinating foreign capital. Her activities during her layover are dependent on how much she accomplished at home during the previous few days. If there are thank-you notes to write or bills to be paid, you will find Liz in her hotel room with her checkbook on the desk, eating a room service dinner. But when she is in London, her favorite layover city, she goes to the theater—Shakespeare outdoors if it's summertime—eats Indian food, and peruses her favorite clothing store, where she can get something special for herself or the children. "A trip to London would not be complete without a stop and shop at Harrods," says Liz.

In the before-children days, Liz couldn't wait to get out to see the sights whenever and wherever she had a layover in Europe. In fact, during a trip to Madrid in January 1994, when all of her friends refused to go sightseeing, she boldly asked a pilot to tour the city with her. "Let's get some espresso," she suggested while on the bus from the plane to the terminal. That pilot turned out to be Pete Campbell, her future husband.

Yet even with perfect planning, having Mom in the air and Dad on the ground, there are always unexpected glitches. As travelers, we have all experienced them, from weather delays to equipment problems. So like all other working couples, the Campbells have a backup plan which, fortunately, they have had to use only a couple of times. When they lived in Florida, a friend came over to stay with the children. In Texas, when they are in a pinch, they send Liz's dad an airline ticket and he flies up to Dallas from San Antonio.

When we first spoke to Liz in the winter of 2003, she was on an "overage leave" from American Airlines for six months, with another six months to go. At a time when the airline industry was suffering, American offered "overage leave" as a cost-cutting method, enticing workers to take time off without pay but accruing vacation time and seniority, with the anticipation of returning to work. Liz looks forward to going back because she thinks she has a great job. "I do miss my flying. I miss the layovers, the adult conversations, the simple me-time that I don't get being a full-time mom. It is such a reprieve and I get energized. It is just enough time away from home."

Perhaps one of the unexpected perks of the girl ghetto jobs is that long after child care is a concern, the work and the camaraderie still offer much satisfaction. "According to a survey of time usage, the teachers who put in the longest hours were over age fifty. They love their work so much they don't go home early and they enjoy a healthy social life at work," notes Dr. Robert Drago, professor of labor studies and women's studies at Pennsylvania State University. You'll find most nurses and flight attendants feel the same about their jobs. They make lifelong friends with whom they work and play. Going to work means being with your friends. So don't let anyone discourage you by speaking disparagingly of "women's work." Not when it translates to rewarding careers with lots of social interaction, flexible hours, and decent pay and benefits that can accommodate your changing lifestyle over the decades.

A DOZEN JOBS YOU NEVER THOUGHT OF, WITH A NOD TO THE WOMEN IN THIS BOOK FOR BEING SO CREATIVE

1. Résumé writer
2. Telephone triage nurse
3. Recreational center science instructor
4. Episcopal priest
5. Trauma counselor
6. Physicians' compliance officer
7. Community recreation director
8. Corporate events planner
9. Dolphin trainer
10. Author escort
11. Virtual office owner
12. Art therapist

Four

Starting Your Own Business

THE NUMBERS ARE STAGGERING: One out of every eighteen women is a business owner.[1] There are an estimated 10.1 million majority-owned, privately held, women-owned firms in the United States, generating $2.3 trillion in sales and 18.2 million jobs. From a home-based crocheted toilet-paper-cover business to a major manufacturing plant, more than eighteen million women in the United States are employed by woman-owned companies.[2]

It's easy to understand why women want to start a business. What mom hasn't thought, "It would be great to be my own boss"? But before you take the dive financially, emotionally, and intellectually into the exciting world of entrepreneurship, ask yourself, "Why do I want to be in my own business?" Is it because you couldn't imagine answering to anyone after being the queen bee at home for so long? Have you been sitting on a clever business idea for years, waiting for the children to get older to see if you can make it work? Are you sick and tired of *Sesame Street* or MTV—depending on your kids' ages—and looking for some adult stimulation? Or do you see starting your own business as an intellectual challenge and you are ready to meet it head-on?

It is important to focus on the reason you want to go into business for yourself. Write down the reason(s) in your agenda. Now use the writer's technique that we use: Read what you wrote out loud. Listen to how it sounds. If a friend told you that she was starting a business for this same reason, would you think she had a great idea, or would you think she had had one too many martinis? If your reasoning still sounds realistic and feasible after hearing it aloud, start thinking about the other important questions. Is this going to be a full-time or part-time job? Seasonal or year-round? At home or out in an office? Some women want to start small but dream about building their business through the years. Suddenly you are talking about bankers and financing and payrolls and a raft of complications and rewards. Like exercising, there are various degrees of dedication and intensity. A stroll in the park a few days a week is enough exercise for some; for others, walking on a treadmill; for still others, a triathlon is the workout of choice. Are you willing to be on call 24/7, in the hope that that your business will soar, or is a tortoise pace better suited to your lifestyle? Remember, you are the boss and the staff; you answer to no one; you make all the decisions; you alone reap the rewards . . . or deal with the failure.

Starting at Home

Some 3.5 million women own home-based businesses, accounting for 66 percent of all such businesses.[4] For many women, there's no place like home . . . as a workplace. No rent, no commute, no business wardrobe, and you can be hands-on at three P.M. when the children come home. The major downside is that motivation, discipline, praise, and camaraderie will all have to come from you. For some, working alone is nirvana: no personalities to deal with; set your own pace; blast Bach or Bruce Springsteen! The fantasy may seem wonderful but the reality does not suit everyone. One in four of home-based business owners misses the financial security, the benefits, and the interaction with coworkers, according to the American Association of Home-Based Businesses.[5]

Home-based businesses are not new to any of us. From garage sales to Tupperware parties, many moms tried their hand at some sort of home-based business when their children were small. As children get older, they are ready to start more ambitious home-based businesses. We are happy to report that almost 70 percent of women's home-based businesses survive three years or more.[6] And these female entrepreneurs truly understand what family-friendly means. They are quick to offer their employees flexible schedules, job sharing, contract work, and profit sharing. While they employ 5.6 million full-time workers, there are 8.4 million people who work for these businesses part-time or contractually.[7] It's not surprising that these employers allow early in/early out, and understand two hours away from the office for a recital or an elderly parent's medical appointment.

While home-based business seems like a manageable way to go, many new business owners are choosing the riskier venture outside the home. In fact, the greatest growth in women-owned businesses in recent years is in construction, manufacturing, and transportation, although service and retail still make up the largest share. To some women, the whole point of starting your own business is to get out of the house—perhaps build on all that expertise you learned on the job BC, perhaps spin off a profit-making venture from your volunteer work, perhaps look at another company and decide, "I could do that better and smarter."

There are many factors to consider before you start beautifying the basement for your office or banging down the bankers' doors. Adding children complicates the equation. In our search for women business owners who had been there, done that and could share the lessons leaned, we found an incredible range of moms, some already mentioned in this book, from the women who started Flexible Resources, to career counselors, to résumé writers, to literary agents. In this chapter, the moms range from an events coordinator in Michigan who works ten hours a week, to a steel fabricator in Alabama with customers including Armani and the army. The common denominator: They wanted to be the boss and say, "I did it my way." What makes these women fascinating is their range of approaches, from a business dropping in one mom's lap, to a long struggle to find a profitable business, to trying to start a manufacturing business, to working with a husband and surviving to tell the story. Think of these micro–case studies as a quick course in entrepreneurship.

If you wonder whether you have the drive and stamina to make it in your own business, take a look at this checklist. "Ten Traits Shared by Winners"[8] outlines some of the unique qualities of entrepreneurs. The U.S. Small Business Administration's Online Women's Business Center at www.onlinewbc.gov is an excellent resource for anyone who wants to be her own boss.

Ten Traits Shared by Winners

1. **An eye for opportunity**: You find a need and fill it.
2. **Independence:** You enjoy being your own boss.
3. **An appetite for hard work:** You are willing to work long hours with little pay.
4. **Self-confidence:** You possess the self-confidence needed to cope with all the risks of operating your own business.
5. **Discipline:** You can resist the temptation to do what is the easiest and have the ability to focus on the essentials.
6. **Judgment:** You are able to think quickly and make wise decisions.
7. **Ability to accept change:** You thrive on changes.
8. **Make stress work for you:** You are able to focus on the end result, not the process of getting there.
9. **Need to achieve:** For you, profits are sometimes secondary in the drive toward personal success.
10. **Focus on profits:** However, you also know that business success is measured by profits.

Starting Small

Many women start working at home as contractors; some work independently, others as employees. A company provides them with the work, they perform the task and, voilà, added income. Everyone is happy. That's how Lisa Roberts of Fairfield, Connecticut, started as a data entry operator. It sounded like win-win. She could work from home six hours a day and be provided with a computer at a time before most people had their own PCs. "They actually paid per stroke," Lisa said. "The faster you typed, the more you made, and I typed one hundred words a minute."

This starter job did something very important for Lisa. It showed her that she could be disciplined, working six hours a day from her home, even with an infant in the house. After a year and the advice of her sister-in-law, who was a pioneer in the computer industry, Lisa decided to be her own boss. Emboldened by a how-to book by start-your-own-business gurus Paul and Sarah Edwards, Lisa bought herself a computer and a laser printer, and she became an entrepreneur with her business, PC Plus. She put up signs at universities, supermarkets, and local stores, offering database management and typing services. Her timing was fortuitous. "Within a year, desktop-publishing software hit, which was a natural for me. I learned that my equipment and skills could compete with the old typesetting methodology that was standard at the time for local printers. I showed them I could create forms, ads, and much more—quickly, meticulously, and cost effectively—and another door swung wide open for me."

Wanting to share her story of the perils and pluses of working at home, she began writing a book while pregnant with her fourth child. "It was an amazing time for me," says Lisa. "No one knew I was writing this book except a very close friend. The book and the baby grew inside me at the same time." In *How to Raise a Family and a Career Under One Roof*,[9] Lisa's message is clear: It is easier to manage when both are in the same location. She also shared advice: Working at home does not mean your children necessarily need to be with you at all times. Lisa opted to take her children to a babysitter three days a week for several hours. Over the following years, Lisa coauthored another book, *The Entrepreneurial Parent*,[10] with the same work-at-home honchos who inspired her years before, Paul and Sarah Edwards. She also started a related Web site, en-parent.com. Lisa says, "Everyone makes choices; every family is different. There is no cookie-cutter way. The point is that a home business is one viable option among many others."

That option may work for a few years or many years. That's one of the upsides of home business. When her youngest went off to first grade, Lisa chose to leave the house too and work ten minutes away as a grant writer in the development office at Fairfield University. She says simply, "All my kids are in school now. It was the right time in my life."

The right time? Does it ever seem like there will be a right time? There's always something happening in the frenetic lives we lead. Children entering a new school, husband starting a new job, moving to a bigger house, caring for an elderly parent, losing your support system. One of the lessons we learned as we talked to dozens of moms is that when opportunity knocks, answer the door! Don't be afraid to stretch out of your comfort zone. If starting an at-home business is an idea swimming around in the back of your mind, be open and ready because opportunities present themselves in the most unexpected times. That's exactly what happened to Beth O'Connor, who was at home in De Pere, Wisconsin, with two small children after working a decade as an event planner. Out of the blue, her former employer called from Boston one day in early 2002. They had a meeting scheduled for Green Bay. Was Beth interested in handling it? "It was right up the road; I could be on-site," Beth says. "I said, 'Sure.' It would be kind of fun."

Beth geared up quickly. FedEx and the fax machine became her buzz words, and during the crunch time, her husband, John, took the children to day care at his company. Beth's business began to grow when John's colleague learned that Beth was an event planner and asked if she would work on an event for their company. "I said, 'I don't want to work,' but I agreed to plan a charity golf event," says Beth. "It turned out to be three hundred hours' worth of work and raised $250,000 for the Boys and Girls Club of Green Bay." After that rip-roaring success, the company was not going to let Beth go. The human resources department asked her to coordinate its coast-to-coast leadership-training series, forty meetings from January to September. Beth is the first to admit that it is not always easy trying to be your best for both clients and children. "Maybe the office floor is not vacuumed and I still have Christmas and Halloween decorations up, but it works for me," she says. "I really enjoy what I do. I feel guilty that I enjoy it so much."

In spite of the out-of-season decorations around her house, Beth seems to have it all under control. She works ten hours a week consistently and accepts the fact that ten turns into forty right before an event. Her clients understand that she is always available two days a week, and she tries to make some calls in the car after she drops off her children, Katherine and Callahan. "I find clients are understanding. I can always do a phone call; they can always reach me. I tell them, 'I can always guarantee you a Monday or Wednesday.'" But she finds that managing the children can be a bit trickier than client control. "The hardest time is first thing in the morning; I can't leave the little guy in the high chair," she says. "He is Houdini." Beth's three-year-old daughter and fifteen-month-old son both understand that a shut door means Mom's working. When all else fails, Beth uses her fool-proof backup system. "I learned that it is very important to have a mute button on the phone because a playroom for the kids is right next to my office," she explains while laughing.

Your Home Business Can Be a Full-Time Job

Many women dream about running their own business, but the question of what kind of business boggles them. Indeed, there's a whole industry built up around helping wannabe business owners figure out where to start. At one such entrepreneurial trade show a few years ago, Kelley Senkowski, from Byron Center, Michigan, in search of a business, learned about Eagle Travel, a company that employs twenty-five hundred independent contractors as travel agents. Kelley jumped on the bandwagon and worked for Eagle for three years, building a remarkable roster of 165 clients. But, like so many others, when her husband was laid off, she had to go back to a full-time, salaried job in management at a travel agency. In exchange for bringing clients with her to the new company, Kelley became a part owner.

"As is usual in my life, things quickly changed," says Kelley. "They wanted me to buy the business. My lawyer posted a red flag and said, 'Go back on your own, go back on your own.' Fortunately, we had signed a contract that said within a period of time, they could get back their equity and I could keep my client list." Heeding her attorney's advice, within nine months Kelley left that travel agency and opened her own travel agency. With three young children and a husband who was starting his own new business, Kelley worked part-time in the evenings. Now the business has grown, and she puts in upward of thirty hours a week.

Any day of the week you can find Kelley in her home, where the lower level has now been converted to the office of Group Tours & Cruises, All One Travel, Inc. Drawing on her sales background, Kelley has conceived of a unique kind of travel business where she works from the top down rather than the bottom up. The business model is simple. She provides the trip—the ship, travel arrangements, and specialist in the field like an author, craftsperson, or historian—and she relies on her agents to provide the clients. She likens her business plan more to a sales company than a travel agency. From conferences on ships to Holy Land tours to marriage enrichment cruises, Kelley talks about volume bookings and wants to capitalize on her sales experience. "I am going after the big fish, concentrating on group tours and cruises," she says. "I am doing the business development. I can sell it. I can organize it. But I need people to implement it so I can go on to sell the next group." All One Travel has already landed one statewide professional organization as a client and a national organization that arranges hundreds of meetings. "I had a sixty-person trip to the Holy Land, but we had to cancel because of travel warnings," she says disappointedly. "It was through three different churches across Michigan where the pastors all knew each other."

Although her business is in its infancy, Kelley is already thinking about the future and bringing in a larger sales staff. She started with only one employee but set up three desks, ready for others. "I foresee having several commissioned sales agents who are serious about what they are doing. They represent my company. If you can sell and talk about what you are doing, you don't need travel experience. You have to have some interest and background in sales."

For those employees who don't know where to look for new business, Kelley has devised her own training programs. She asks her agents, "What are your hobbies? Where do you want to travel to?" If someone says she likes to knit, Kelley follows by asking, "Where do you go to buy the yarn? Okay, put up a flyer in the yarn store." She even offers store managers cash incentives for promoting a tour. "Scrapbooking is huge. Go to a crafts chain and offer the manager a $100 incentive for selling the most trips to a scrapbooking tour on a cruise ship."

Kelley believes she has the best of both worlds. "I feel so much better than I ever did. If I have to take my child to the doctor or if they are home sick, I am around. When we had a whiteout storm, I could get to their school in twenty minutes. That is comforting to me." Kelley's kids—Taylor, Austin, and Morgan—know the drill when Mom is downstairs working. "When I had babies, I would get a high school or college student to help me. I put up a gate. When I shut the gate it's their signal that I am working. For the first time I am at a point in my life where I can work from ten to four."

Like Kelley, Diana LeGere always knew she would someday have a business of her own; the entrepreneurial spirit was in her blood. Everyone in her family owned a business, from a fence company to an electrical repair service to a ceramics studio. The road to launching her company, Executive Final Copy, was a long one, crisscrossing the country, with several small businesses along the way. There was even a dry spell with next to no income during the start-up six months.

Like many women, Diana doesn't forget anything. She learns a skill in one place, then uses it in another. After working in retail management at a Sears Portrait Studio in New York, Diana started her own photography business, Photographs by Diana, specializing in portraits and weddings. Her clients were astounded by her creativity. "I was so poor when I started out that I put cotton balls on the bottom of the lens [as makeshift filters]," says Diana. "It created fabulous results and people were amazed."

When her family moved to Utah, Diana found it difficult to relaunch her photography business because she wasn't permitted into Mormon temples to take wedding photographs. Since her two children were under four at the time, she decided to take five years off to be an at-home mom. But even during those years, Diana was honing her at-home business acumen, starting a number of small businesses, some of which were short-term successes. "I started selling Tupperware, but I think it was something about carrying the big bag that turned me off to that." Pretty Petals, like Photographs by Diana, tapped her creativity. She turned flowers into hand-painted porcelain decorations and put them on jewelry boxes and wreaths. "It was a thing of the moment," says Diana. "It was insignificant but indulged my creative juices. It gave me something to do when the kids were playing with neighbors."

As her children grew, Diana seriously started considering possible new business ventures. One thing was for sure: Working for someone else was never on her radar screen. Diana wanted something to call her own and liked the challenge of starting from square one. She wasn't certain what kind of business she would tackle, but she knew that it was important for her to really love what she was doing. Diana had her own way of testing possible business ideas, asking herself, "What would I be doing if I didn't get paid?" and the answer always involved some kind of writing. "It has to be something I love. Writing is what I have loved my whole life," she concluded. With that goal in mind, she started another new business, Executive Final Copy, an administrative support service company that writes résumés, presentations, and projects. Her motto: "We give words to those who know what they want to say but not how to say it."

Launching Executive Final Copy was not easy. For the first six months, her business brought in $82, so to supplement her next-to-nothing salary, she delivered newspapers from two A.M. to six-thirty. Diana says, "I did it to make my $400-a-month car payment. At six-thirty I would come home and have some coffee and start writing."

Diana eventually took on five newspaper routes and continued delivering papers for two years. She was finally able to give up her "night" job when she got a big break with a large career management firm that outsourced résumé writing. "Sleep was hard to come by," she says. "When it was killing me, I quit delivering newspapers, giving up one route at a time. I didn't really need the money because it was my play money, but I also knew outsource work was not guaranteed income." As the months and years passed, she was able to whip out résumés faster and faster and soon felt comfortable upping her fees. Today, she can write a résumé in a couple of hours, not days, and instead of a $65 fee, she charges her personal clients $350.

Delivering newspapers also gave Diana money to equip her home office. While a well-functioning workplace is important to Diana, she believes that creating a professional image is key. To that end, Diana got a toll-free number, which cost her $20 a month and made her clients feel very secure. Several home-business moms told us it was worth the cost to have a dedicated phone line. One noted, "When I call my clients, the business name appears on their caller ID and to them that means I'm sitting in an office building somewhere, plus I can write off the expense."

Having a successful home business was important to Diana, but she had another personal goal: to be a published writer. To give herself an incentive, she hung a blank piece of paper on her office wall and wrote across the top "publishing credits by Diana LeGere." Her first article was published shortly after opening Executive Final Copy. "I was in that first six months of starving mode, no customers and just trying to keep busy doing something," she says. Today the list of published pieces runs on for three pages, including magazine articles and a column for a local newspaper. Her articles are both practical and inspirational, on topics from résumé paper stock to reaching your personal goals. "What you believe in your mind is what you will get," says Diana. "I believed that paper would become full. I know how to be a positive person and how to be excited about life."

Here are Diana LeGere's five Success Strategies for Starting a Home Business:

1. **Do what you love.** Starting a new business initially demands many long hours. You are much less apt to quit if you enjoy what you are doing.

2. **Research the market.** Loving your work does not guarantee success. Explore the market trends in your region to ensure that your service or product is viable. What works in the city will not necessarily be a big hit in a small town.

3. **Prepare for obstacles.** You will have challenges. Plan ahead and create a backup strategy for potential impediments such as revenue loss, customer service problems, additional expenses, and even a sudden influx of business.

4. **Offer outstanding customer service.** This is a guaranteed revenue booster. If you give more than is expected, customers will come back and they will talk. Referrals are everything. My first customer paid $65 for a résumé. I bought the most expensive black folder, gold labels, plastic sheeting for the presentation. I did everything to make it perfect. My client said, "I didn't expect to get this much." Sometimes I give my clients a really nice pen with my name on it, or planners with a motivational saying.

5. **Keep a positive attitude.** No matter what happens, you will succeed if you focus on your goal. Never be afraid to alter your strategy as needed, and keep moving forward!

Owning Your Own Store

You walk into a perfect little shop. Soothing music plays in the background, a scented candle flickers, one accessory is more beautiful than the next . . . or the pounding music vibrates and the funky clothes jump out at you. You think, "I could do this. I would love to own this shop." But the start-up costs and the licenses and the vendors all seem so overwhelming that the thought passes by the time you're at the register, testing the limits of your charge card. Don't throw away that idea so fast. Lots of businesses start small. Mary knew a woman who made silk flower arrangements and wreaths. First she sold them out of her garage and took phone orders; then she moved to a small shop on an out-of-the-way street; finally she moved to a large store filled with furniture, mirrors, and paintings as well as flowers, located on the main shopping street. Her husband even went to work for her! After owning her business for two decades, she sold the shop to two young women who worked for her and went part-time, joining her son in his interior design business. You never know where the first small step will lead you.

When Kathy Carlson Matulich met a woman selling handbags at her son's school fund-raiser, Kathy invited her and some forty other women to her home for lunch and the handbag equivalent of a Tupperware party. The bags were a big hit, but Kathy's house became the star attraction. It was the oohs and aahs for her exquisite hacienda that propelled Kathy to open Casa Allegra, a Spanish-Mission-and-Mexican-inspired gift store along trendy Main Street in Santa Monica, California. She had been looking for something to do but was not sure what it would be until those rave reviews of her home. "I thought I was going to be a princess. My painter even bought me a tiara," says Kathy, who fashioned Casa Allegra after her own home. "I couldn't get more Botox or just do my Pilates. I had to do something."

Kathy worked as a buyer and a women's clothing representative before she stayed home for nine years, and her sense of style and her eye for design never left her. Today, they are both apparent in every inch of space, upstairs and down, in her dazzling boutique, which specializes in unique gifts and home furnishings. But make no mistake, Casa Allegra may be a labor of love, but it's not easy to run a retail business that depends so much on her imprint. Kathy works from ten to ten, a very long day that has taken its toll on her family and social life. "I was the fun mom," says Kathy, her large silver hoop earrings tossing back and forth as she speaks. "All the kids would come over to our house. And I had all my friends over too. It was the place where everyone gathered. I have no friends anymore because I am here all the time."

But it's easy to see that Kathy has new friends in her life. She gets into lively conversation with each and every customer who saunters through her door, sometimes ignoring the constant ring of the telephone. After she assisted a man looking for a lamp, he helped her figure out how to use her new camera. From fledgling models to stay-at-home moms, all of her customers seem to have their mood elevated as soon as they walk into the shop, eyeing everything from vanilla grapefruit candles, to the wide array of crosses, to the Frida Kahlo red plastic pocketbooks.

Back at the cash register Kathy becomes a bit more stoic. "I always double-check myself," she says. "I have learning disabilities. I used to pride myself that I can do so many things at once and now I found out I have ADD. I truly can't do two things at one time." Then while writing up the invoice, Kathy suddenly realizes what date it is. With a chuckle, she looks up and says, "It's my sister's birthday today. I own a gift store and I didn't give her anything!"

Starting a Business with Your Husband

Here is a far-out idea: Start a business with your husband. Some are saying, "No way." While this may not be for everybody, it sure works for the Boyd and Caruso family, from Roswell, Georgia, an Atlanta suburb. They didn't plan to work together, but it seemed the perfect blending of two sets of skills: her knowledge of marketing and technology sales and his of technology and business development. Together they make the perfect pair to run a boutique PR firm that specializes in technology clients.

Becky Boyd left Hewlett Packard, where she had sold engineering systems for thirteen years, after she adopted her son. She couldn't see how a job that required crisscrossing the state of Georgia, monthly trips to headquarters in California, and twelve-hour days meshed with motherhood. Becky stayed home until her son entered kindergarten. Her husband was managing the Atlanta office of a Cleveland, Ohio, public relations firm. "I was clueless about PR," she says. "I didn't know about media relations and client relations. Watching my husband, I realized it takes sales skills and a sense of the market. Jim would bring home his work and I would see what he was doing." After an initial reentry job didn't work out, she thought about joining her husband. "I told him, 'This is what I want to do. I understand technology. I sold it in the manufacturing environment at HP. It is a natural fit. You need to hire me. Hire me, hire me, hire me.'"

Sometimes our nagging pays off. Jim bought the Atlanta office and Becky began working in their downtown office, still making certain she was home to be with their son at three-fifteen. "This is stupid," she told Jim one day, as she was hurrying home. "We have this really nice basement in our house and we are paying rent." So the Caruso/Boyds decided to outfit their basement for the business. "Some people say, 'I could never work with my husband.' We work in different rooms. He has his strengths; he is the visionary and has the entrepreneurial vision and spirit. I am more tactical, doing the media relations and getting placements for clients in the media." Do they take their business to the dinner table? "Sometimes," Becky says, but she answers with a decisive no when asked if it ever gets into the bedroom.

"It was the perfect decision for me and our family, and it helped raise my self-esteem and self-confidence. The business is doing great. I think the dot-com bust has helped us. A lot of companies have laid off their PR and marketing people, but they see the value for what those services provide." Becky doesn't advertise to their clients that she and Jim are husband and wife; in fact, she uses her maiden name for business. Eventually their clients learn that they are married. When they were on a trip to California, Jim brought along his laptop computer, from which Becky checked and sent e-mail, not realizing that her name was coming across as her married name, Becky Caruso. After receiving an e-mail from Becky, one client called her to say, "Congratulations, I see you two got married."

Husband-and-wife partnerships are nothing new. However, in the old days, pop was the boss and mom took the orders. No longer. Today husbands and wives like Becky and Jim bring their own skill sets to the business partnership, putting them on equal footing. But for some couples, finding a balance of power can be tricky. It's important to identify responsibilities and areas of expertise before going in.

The twenty-first-century version of a mom-and-pop business

can be found in a suburban office park in Charlotte, not far from the University of North Carolina. Susan and Bob Feezor run ExecuBusiness Centers, twenty thousand square feet of contemporary furnished offices and meeting rooms with a full range of administrative and clerical support services. Beautifully decorated with plants and prints, the sleek offices are welcoming, from the reception area with four clocks marking different time zones—California, Charlotte, India, and Malaysia—to a sunny conference room seating fifty people, with catered lunch if desired.

ExecuBusiness Centers provides office space and services by the hour or the year, and its clients range from a four-person Web design company, to out-of-town lawyers who need space twice a month to meet with local clients, to salespeople who work out of their cars and require a mail drop and a telephone answering service. Other clients include CPA moms who usually work from home but need office space during tax season so that children aren't running circles around clients, two lawyers from other cities in North Carolina who meet local clients, and a New York–based medical research company.

The business draws on the experiences of both partners. Bob was a senior vice president for information systems at BellSouth, and Susan worked part-time as an administrative assistant for fifteen years while raising their three children. The Feezors had always dreamed of owning their own business but instead opted for the security of Bob's position with the telephone company. When Bob, along with hundreds of other employees, was downsized in the mid-1990s, the couple saw it as an opportunity to make their dream a reality.

While Susan says that she and Bob have a good working relationship, she offers some learned-the-hard-way advice for women contemplating going into business with hubby. "I think you should consider your husband's personality and position in business. My husband was always the boss, used to having people working for him. Anytime he did not want to do something he'd pass it off to his staff, but when we first started his staff was just me! But I saw myself as his partner."

Eventually Susan and Bob settled on his-and-her duties. Not surprisingly, Bob handles all computer and other technological tasks, and Susan oversees all the administrative work. They also discovered that while Bob is good at closing the deal with new clients, Susan's strong suit is the ongoing client contact, which helps generate repeat business. Susan suggests that couples have a no-holds-barred discussion about the division of labor and that they actually write down each partner's responsibility. When it comes to budgets, Susan also recommends putting it in writing to lessen chances of a dispute later. "Sometimes he wanted new equipment, like a server for the computer, and I wanted to spend the money another way." Sound advice for any partners, married or not.

The couple took a methodical approach before spending their hard-earned savings. Bob spent a year thoroughly researching business possibilities. They narrowed down the choices to three options, including insurance and home security, before deciding on a company that leases office space and business services. Using their savings, Bob and Susan leased space in an office complex not far from their home in July 1998, starting as part of a franchise. After a year of sixty-hour weeks, the Feezors decided they would be better off on their own and left the franchise. Susan admits it was nerve-racking, with their savings invested in the business, working long hours, trying to get clients, and having two children at home. Her only regret: "I should have done it sooner."

They built their business through advertisements, word of mouth, even small signs on the highway announcing "Executive Office and Conference Space" for rent. Their business, with a staff of three assistants, is now a success, and they recently added a large conference room to accommodate several local companies that have chosen video teleconferencing rather than executive travel. In part their success comes from delivering on promises to their clients, but Susan also credits the personal touch. For instance, to make a regular client feel like it's her own office, even for just a few hours a month, Susan has a nameplate made and puts it on the door when the client is "in."

Susan cautions that starting a business always has hidden costs and suggests building unexpected extras into the budget. From an interior landscape service to dishwashing detergent to flowers for clients, there are things both big and small that are overlooked when you open a new business. "We ended up taking a second mortgage on our house plus using some of Bob's retirement funds to get up and going. I recommend that anyone thinking of going into their own business do very thorough research about the field. Make sure they have an idea about what they can afford. Those little things can suddenly add up to a lot of money."

Working with your husband requires special handling, says Ira Bryck, director of the UMass Family Business Center. He offers these points to keep in mind:

- The motto for Ira's center is "Treat Your Business Like a Business and Your Family Like a Family." Limit business talk to a designated time and don't let it spill into your personal life.
- Focus on your special talents, not just job skills. Split tasks according to your personal strengths, not gender stereotypes.
- Decide how you are going to share power and credit for a job well done. It helps to develop a one-for-all-and-all-for-one attitude.
- Figure out how decisions will be made when you and your husband disagree. Who casts the tie-breaking vote? Even a small business benefits from a board of advisers, or at least regular meetings with your professional service providers, discussing your agenda.
- Keep romance in the relationship by blocking off time for the two of you as a couple, not business partners. Even if you are great business partners, working with someone you love is more fun.
- Make sure you are going into your own business to pursue a passion. Otherwise you might as well lessen the stress and work for someone else.

Starting a Business Without Your Husband . . . But with His Advice

When Carolyn Minerich, a fifty-year-old mom and former U.S. Marine from Jacksonville, Alabama, told her husband that she wanted to do something but wasn't quite sure in which direction to go, Jon came up with an idea. "My husband said, 'Find a machine that no one else has in the area.' He planted the seed and I ran with it."

Jon believed that Carolyn, who was in the Marine Corps from 1973 to 1978, could do anything she set her mind to. "In starting a business, I combined everything I learned as a Marine Corps officer and my passion for educating young people," she says. Between her years in the marines and starting her company, Carmin Industries, Carolyn brought these same skills and values to her "job" as a hands-on, at-home mom. She loved teaching her son, Jon Jr., and daughter, Cathy, who were both reading by the time they were three and doing long division in first grade. Carolyn even contemplated teaching her children a foreign language, but since she wasn't fluent in any, she taught them sign language instead.

It was always Carolyn's intention to return to school when her kids went to college, but with the high cost of tuition looming ahead, returning to work was more practical. When the children were both in high school, Carolyn decided to explore work options.

It took more than a nudge from her husband to get the business off the ground. Jon had read about water-jet cutting technology, where water, under sixty thousand pounds of pressure, is pushed through a hole a sixteenth of an inch in diameter to cut many materials, including steel, granite, marble, and glass. At his suggestion, Carolyn started researching more about the process as well as how to start a small business. It didn't take her long to realize that if she was going to start a business, the first things she needed were money and a building. Armed with a business plan and gumption, she went off to see some local bankers. Unfortunately, the encouragement that she got from Jon was tempered by the bankers' discouragement. Her meetings went something like this:

Banker:	Have you ever done this before?
Carolyn:	No.
Banker:	Do you have any customers?
Carolyn:	No.
Banker:	Have you ever been in manufacturing?
Carolyn:	No, but having spent five years in the Marine Corps, there is nothing that I can't do.

At this point some of the bankers actually escorted Carolyn to her car, opened the door, and waited until she was down the street . . . out of sight!

So how did Carolyn get her seed money to start this new business? Because of the solid sense of confidence she gained as a marine, Carolyn was not ready to wave the white flag. One bank after another turned her down until she finally went into Compass Bank in Anniston, Alabama. To her surprise, the banker at Compass had read about the water-jet process and was intrigued. A little bit of luck and a lot of perseverance landed Carolyn the loan she needed, and in 1996, Carmin Industries was born. The bank money was key, but Carolyn recommends that any woman contemplating a new business venture visit the local Small Business Development Office for help. Besides suggesting banks, they helped her locate a building and even found her Carmin Industries' first employees.

Today, Carmin has twenty-two employees, all key to the success of her company. Carolyn is particularly proud of the young people who work for her. Through the years she has gotten to know teachers at both Jacksonville High School and Jacksonville State University. They send special students her way, like Pete Hudson, a high school senior whom Carolyn both employs and mentors. "He is smart, bright, and scared to death. He said, 'Please don't make me answer the phone,' so guess what he is doing," says Carolyn with a chuckle. Pete is just one of a long list of employees she has helped start along a career path.

It has not always been easy for Carolyn as a woman in a macho-man business, but once again, the marines taught her how to hold her own. When she was doing a project that required cutting large steel panels for Giorgio Armani's boutique in the Beverly Hills Neiman Marcus store, she needed help from a machine shop to complete the job. She took her daughter with her to a local machine shop where she got a less-than-warm reception. "They laughed at me," says Carolyn. "They would not help me, and some very unkind things were said to me. It's a double-edged sword: a woman in business in the South. You have to take a deep breath and forget about it. I told myself I have to be successful. I owe it to these bank people."

While Carolyn was not happy that this happened, she was glad that her daughter saw her mom pull herself up by the bootstraps. She also sees that her mom works hard and often has very long days. Carolyn doesn't load the trucks or work the machinery anymore, but her workday runs from "whenever to whenever." Typically rising at four-thirty, she takes a mile walk every morning to clear her head and gets into the office at six-thirty, never taking time for lunch.

The Carmin Industries' slogan says it all: "If you can dream it, we can cut it." Because Carmin is willing to tackle what others might consider impossible, its customers represent a cross section of American business, from Estée Lauder to Universal Studios to the Smithsonian. With this roster of A-list clients and the company prospering, it's hard not to wonder if Carolyn's husband, Jon, a manufacturing consultant who advises other companies world-wide, might jump ship and join the ranks of Carmin Industries. "We would kill each other if we were in business together," Carolyn says. "You can see how much help he is to me, when I decide to listen to him," she says with a chuckle. "Evidently the advice he is giving me works."

As she sees companies crumbling around her, Carolyn has every intention of expanding her business, setting her sights high. She projects that two-thirds of her business will be defense contract work—"that's where the money is"—and she still dreams about landing a million-dollar contract. "Isn't it amazing how life turns out?" Carolyn asks rhetorically. "I am having more fun now than I ever have. A woman can make the impact and still be feminine and still be a very strong woman. I want to be an example for one woman every day."

Job Sharing Your Own Company

For some women, owning a full-time business requires just too much juggling. So why not combine two ideas? Start your own business and job-share like Houston moms Mary Ann Loweth and Becky Stewart. Mary Ann may look like a soccer mom driving around Houston and its sprawling suburbs in her TV-equipped Suburban. But don't be fooled; her family-friendly vehicle is used not only for car pooling the kids. These days Mary Ann, a former aide to a U.S. senator, uses her car to take visiting book authors around the city to TV and radio stations and bookstores. Their company is called Expressly Yours, Inc.

Mary Ann's initiation into the author escort business was serendipitous. A stay-at-home mom, she received a call one day from a woman whom she knew from politics, asking her to escort author Mary Higgins Clark to appointments in the Houston area. Mary Ann assumed that it was a one-day job, but a few months later she got another call, and then another. With two small children at home, Mary Ann continued to accept occasional assignments. "I thought this was a unique opportunity to be a full-time mom and keep my finger in something," she says.

As her occasional business grew into a steady stream of authors, and as another baby came along, Mary Ann needed help and decided that job sharing was the answer. Her current partner, Becky Stewart, was a former college classmate whom she bumped into at a Mommy & Me group. "We started with a phone in a large interior closet," says Becky. "The rule was that when Mommy was in the closet you could not bother her. Mary Ann and I acted like the international world headquarters of a Fortune 500 company, but we were really two housewives with an office on my dining room table and in a closet."

That was eighteen years ago, and the "little sideline" has grown to where the pair is busy several days a week, often from six A.M., when an author is picked up at the airport for an early morning news show, to ten P.M. after a bookstore signing. Sometimes the job involves preparing food for a cooking demonstration if the assignment is with a cookbook author, or securing a dog into an airplane cargo compartment. "I tell people my job is the same as being a mother: We service, nurture, and drive our children, and that is what you do with authors," says Mary Ann. "We facilitate their day so that they are calm and relaxed for the five minutes on the TV show to promote a book. Authors shouldn't have to worry about anything."

The partnership has worked because the pair balances each other. "She and I each do what the other detests," says Becky, laughing. "She's very good at doing the billings. I do the bookings, which she has no interest in. I also do all the telephone work to solicit business. She was content to see what came in the door, and for years I chased every tour until we could count on repeat business." So the hours are long and sometimes sporadic and the gas bills are out of sight, but who better to get stuck with in a Houston traffic jam than Dominick Dunne or Richard Simmons?

Lisa Roberts, founder of The Entrepreneurial Parent (visit their Web site at www. en-parent.com), lists these three stumbling blocks to avoid:

- **Don't act against your personality type**. Don't try to be someone you are not. Just because your friend tells you that it's "no sweat" working and watching the kids at the same time, that doesn't mean it will work for you. Lisa suggests figuring out if you are an "integrator" or a "segregator." "If you are good at multitasking and can weave household, child care, and business tasks throughout your day, then you are an integrator. It is a holistic lifestyle. A segregator needs a block of work time and a block of kids' time."

- **Don't try to do too much in your new business.** When Lisa started PC Plus, she intentionally gave her company a generic name so she could take on all sorts of computer projects, but in hindsight she believes that it is better to start with a narrower focus.

- **Leave the guilt behind.** "You feel like you are not all the parent you can be or all the entrepreneur you can be," says Lisa. "Don't feel guilty. Give yourself permission to be who you are."

Five

The Family Challenge

When I told my two teenage sons that I was returning to teaching after a decade-long absence, they complained, "But we'll be latchkey children." I told them, "No, you'll be latchkey adults!"

—Joan Waldman

THE LONG-ANTICIPATED SEPTEMBER morning finally arrives when your youngest child heads off to a full day of school. Now that you have six solid hours sans kids, your mind starts racing. You feel you're ready to go back to work but . . . hmm, maybe the thought of a third child is still stuck in the back of your mind, or what about the great American novel you dreamed about writing?

Big decision: Yes. Making it alone: No. If you think returning to work is up to only you, think again. As much as you might want to fly solo, you can't. Your husband and children are along for the ride too. The first time your career choice was your own. This time each member of your family thinks he or she has voting rights, like a shareholder in a public company called MOM.

You may be pleasantly surprised that your husband is supportive. Some women in our survey commented that their husbands turned into superdad or actually enjoyed cooking dinner. Besides, that extra income may look good to him as the tots turn to teens and sneakers now cost $75, not $25. Indeed, almost 90 percent of the survey women said their husbands were supportive of their return to work. At least that's in theory. Then reality sets in when you're calling from the office to say you need to work late and Dad is the one juggling homework, dinner, and basketball practice. So before you fill out that grad school application or update your résumé, it's best to sit down and have a heart-to-heart with your husband about what life will really be like when you return to work. Only you truly know what goes on during the day with the house and the children. It's hard to imagine not being there. Who will pick up the slack? We know that moms are the best multitaskers around, but don't assume that you will just be adding a new job to everything else you do. We can guarantee that if you don't get help—from inside the house as well as outside—the resentment will boil faster than a mug of water in the microwave.

Even if you are working "just part-time," as many women say, you need to discuss with your husband how his help around the house will, shall we say, improve . . . increase . . . start? Choose your words carefully! It may be as simple as asking your husband to take the children to school or day care a few mornings a week, or making sure he can be there at the end of the day to pick them up. Don't impose the game plan on him. Work on it together. What can he do to make some adjustments to his work schedule?

Staci Handschuh's husband is a New York City newspaper photographer with unpredictable hours, but he often drives hours late at night to get home so she can run a youth program on Saturday mornings.

Maybe it's impossible to get home at a certain time every day, but can he manage two days? Maybe he can grocery shop or hit the wholesale club. Maybe his job is so demanding or constrained that he can't help at all. If so, that should be out in the open and considered fully before you go back, to avoid a civil war!

Hallelujah! Some men finally understand how much their wives do for the family when they are forced into service. "My husband has to take on a lot of things he never did before, like picking kids up, taking them to doctors' appointments, making phone calls to places like the insurance company where you can spend hours on the phone, and other things I always did before," says a mother of two who works as an HR assistant. "He admits he appreciates me."

Before that first paycheck comes in you also need to discuss how it will be spent. Maybe a mountain of accumulated debt needs to be attacked or a college tuition fund needs some more funds. Again it is essential that you calculate your net income (use one of the worksheets for after-expenses income found on the Web) and how it will be spent. When Jaye Hersh, a mother of two from Los Angeles, thought ahead about her children going to college and the additional expense, she opened up a women's clothing store appropriately called Intuition.

Sadly, sometimes your salary is less than you expected because you are working part-time, took a job with more flexibility but less money, or are starting on the ground floor of a new career. Kathryn Sollmann, a cofounder of Women@Work, says some moms tell her that their husbands even belittle how much—or little—they will make after taxes, child care, and clothing. "Women can't focus on that," she says. "The fact is that they may not make a lot of green dollars in the first few years, but if they plan carefully and find flexible work, they can, for example, work during school hours and avoid child-care expenses. And you can't underestimate the value of psychic dollars that cash-in as personal fulfillment."

While your husband most probably will see the upside, it's your children who most likely will feel forsaken and abandoned. Returning to the workforce means being absent from the home front. Sure, there are beepers and cell phones, but Mom will no longer be hands-on 24/7. In response to our survey question, "How did your children feel when you told them you were going back to work?" more than one-third of the moms answered "Deserted." So how do you turn that perception around? Even if you don't plan to return for a year or so, slowly start talking about your plans. Let your children participate in the discussion when possible. This is not to say that they should have input on every issue, but at least solicit their opinion on matters that will affect them directly. We have all heard the adage, "Keep open the lines of communication," and this is one of those times when it is crucial, says Dr. Kristin Moore, president of Child Trends, a Washington D.C.–based research organization. "There should be a lot of communication about your going back. This should not be presented as a fait accompli."

Lisa Roberts, the mother of four children, has worked at home and in a university development office, and she suggests holding a family meeting. "Tell your family, 'This is what I need to do. I want it to work. I need your cooperation. I don't want you to feel that I will not be there for what's important to you.' If you talk directly to kids, they will respect you."

Making Your Case

Talking about going back to work and actually picking a starting date are very different. Breaking the news is a big hurdle. You have only one shot at it, so think carefully about your tactics. You might take your family out for a fast-food dinner as the prototype of what lies ahead. "You like it here?" Mom says. "Oh, yes," is the collective response. "Good," she says, "because this is where we will be every Tuesday night, now that I will be working four days a week." What if this tactic doesn't work and they still make you feel guilty? Get used to it!

Seriously, think about it from your children's perspective. Make a list of the ways their lives will change, so you can better understand why they may not jump for joy when you break the news. You may not be in the schoolyard or at the bus stop to greet them. You might not be home for breakfast. You may need to work late. You won't be sitting in the car waiting after soccer practice. Their routines may change, and no amount of spin will convince them otherwise.

Surprisingly, sometimes it's easier for younger children to comprehend the tangible upside of Mom returning to work. "Why is mommy working?" asks the three-year-old daughter of event planner Beth O'Connor. Beth explains that the money she makes helps buy things like the big play gym in the backyard. Case closed. The economic argument might appeal to teens too. As Dr. Moore notes, one of the best ways to scale the emotional wall that teens erect is to be very supportive of their interests, whether it's a sport, a hobby, or an academic subject. And as anyone who has ever paid thousands of dollars for a sports camp or a new guitar will attest, that "support" often does not come cheaply. "Let them know that is one of the reasons you are working, so you can afford those expensive camps and lessons," said Dr. Moore. Don't be afraid to admit, "We're not rich and Mom needs to work to afford these extras." One mother of three put it simply to her children: "You want a new computer? Mom has to work."

Again, just as with your husband, when you sit down with the children, let them know they will have to pitch in and help out. How will their lives change? When Elaine Levine went back to work full-time as a molecular biologist, her daughters were in elementary, middle, and high school. The plan was for the oldest two to alternate coming home right after school to watch the youngest until Dad arrived at four P.M. "The older two girls had to make arrangements so I knew one of them was always there. They never really complained, perhaps because I left it to them to work out whose turn it was. The one in high school considered it an advantage that I was gone," said Elaine, laughing.

As we know from our conversations, money is not the only reason we return to work. Don't hesitate to tell your children that "it's mom's turn" after the years of staying home. We have all joked in exasperation, "Who do my kids think I am? The maid and chauffeur?" This is a good time to change that perception and to let your children see you in a different light, in a role other than Mom, as someone who may actually know something about life beyond the home. One mom, a former banker who returned to school to become a nurse, told us her three boys could never understand why anyone would ever go to school voluntarily or study so hard. But they did gradually come to realize that she wanted school and work for her own sense of accomplishment.

Obviously, a lot of this conversation depends on children's ages. Preschoolers often seem to have trouble with Mom being gone full-time. Those first few months were very painful, says Kathryn Poling, the Defense Department labor lawyer, describing a move from Colorado back to Washington, D.C. "The kids would cry and hang on to my leg. They would constantly ask why Mommy had to go to work. These kids are smart as whips, and even at three and a half my oldest could meet a lot of my arguments, such as we needed the money for the house. His argument was how did we pay for our house in Colorado? I explained that we used some of Daddy's savings. He wanted to know why we couldn't continue to use Daddy's savings." Her answer? Houses are a lot more expensive in Washington.

Many women wait until their children are in elementary school to go back. At least they are present and accounted for from nine to three. Perhaps your child will enroll in an after-school program or come home to a babysitter. While addressing the reality of a changed routine, you still have to sell it to your children. Maybe there are friends and fun activities and trips in the after-school program. Maybe that babysitter is a "cool" high school or college student who plays with the children. Mary's daughter adored the high school girl who watched her a few afternoons a week over a period of four years. Jeanine was always welcomed because she played games in the backyard and painted toenails and dressed Barbies.

We do not pretend to be experts on day care vs. nanny vs. go it alone. There is a lot of conflicting advice on how to choose child care. What's more, from talking to hundreds of women, we have found there are many variations on a theme. In some situations, one arrangement may work for a long period of time; other situations call for constant tinkering. One mom told us about a beloved babysitter, now regarded as a grandmother, who started when the mom went back part-time. It worked well because the sitter had school-age children of her own and didn't want full-time work. The arrangement continued for more than two decades, as the mom gradually took on full-time work. There were no longer any babies, but the sitter monitored homework, drove to afterschool activities, and started dinner. The mom credits the success to a good personality fit, generous pay, and always treating the sitter with respect. Other moms depend on after-school programs. As several pointed out in our survey, the children usually do their homework during the program, so that when they are picked up it's downtime and less stress on the family.

The best situation is the one where you feel your children are safe, physically and emotionally. This is one time when precision planning is essential. "The critical thing before going back is to make sure that you have the right kind of support in terms of your partner, that your kids are in the right place, and that you have enough outside help," says Dr. Laraine Zappert, a Stanford University psychologist and author of *Getting It Right*.[1]

There's an old Yiddish proverb: "Man plans. God laughs." Sometimes, even though we meticulously map out our lives, suddenly we can spin out of control, with our children caught in the upheaval as well. As an Episcopal priest, Brenda Overfield has seen that proverb in action. At one point all her plans for school and work and life seemed to be synchronized. Then she was turned down for a seminary program and her husband was transferred.

Before she knew it she was in another state, seemingly at loose ends. Almost as fast, she enrolled in General Theological Seminary in New York City, separated from her husband, and moved into the seminary living quarters with her three sons, ages ten, seven, and five. The changes caused havoc with the boys.

Now their home was a 175-year-old seminary, and the boys wandered from rooftop to subtunnels. Brenda tried to get to the root of their acting out and discovered that they were unhappy because Mom, who previously had been home all day, was now in school herself. It didn't matter that the school was on the same sprawling campus in Manhattan's Chelsea. Many other moms also told us that when they initially went back to work, their children were upset because of a lost sense of security with Mom at work instead of in the house. Brenda's children felt this way even though they themselves were gone from nine to three. She decided it was time for a heart-to-heart talk, and one evening she sat down with her sons. She recalls, "I asked them, 'Do you want me to stay at home alone while you are at school? You are safe in your school. Isn't it selfish to want me to stay in the house and just wait for you to come home? I am always here for dinner. We still do all the after-school and evening activities. What is it that you are missing by me being in school while you're in school too?' I think they finally understood when I put it that way."

Keep in mind as you prepare to go back to work that during those years at home you established incredible bonds with your children, and those bonds do not disappear because you are now gone from the house. Perhaps we have to work a little harder at keeping them strong and planning time together rather than relying on impromptu events. Vicki King noted this in an e-mail, "I think that the years spent home with my kids when they were little let me really know their personalities. I know exactly where they have been and what has happened to them every day for the first years. I know how they respond to adversity and excitement. I hope that will be a lifeline between us as I go off to work and they explore life without me right there next to them."

FROM THE GOING BACK SURVEY

Household chores aside, what's the biggest problem balancing family and work?

36 percent: Lack of time for self
23 percent: Lack of time for children
20 percent: Lack of time for husband (to say nothing of a sex life)
13 percent: Tight finances
8 percent: Workplace stress

Other comments: all of the above; aging parents; feeling rushed; the little extras like baking cookies and sewing Halloween costumes; too tired to recall them!

The "G" Word

Even with the best planning you still find that you are dragging around a ball and chain called guilt. Mary's daughter still asks every Tuesday and Thursday, "Are you going to work today?" Yes, Mary is, just as she has done for the past ten years. Does she feel guilty? Yes, for thirty seconds. She has gotten so used to feeling guilty at times that it doesn't nag at her for too long. It seems to be a universal mantra among children: Do you have to work today? "When I worked at the storefront travel agency, I got it all the time," says Kelley Senkowski. The guilt can weigh heavily on us at times. Kathy Carlson Matulich talks about it while trying to handle two ringing phone lines in Casa Allegra, her charming home accessories store. "Emotionally it is a lot to deal with," she says. "It is not Jewish guilt and it is not Catholic guilt. It is a mother's guilt. It is all-consuming when it is your own."

Guilt has become the catchall word for a range of emotions from casual culpability to feeling heartsick. Becky Boyd went back to work—the first time—when her husband was looking for a new job. Her son, Wil, was just one year old. "The guilt was overwhelming," she says. "When my husband got a new job, I left mine immediately." Anything less than being the perfect parent 24/7 seems to leave us with a knot in our stomachs. "There are so many times I feel guilty," says labor lawyer Kathryn Poling. "I really feel like I am the best teacher for my children. I'm not a great playmate, that's their dad, but I am a good teacher. The oldest has been sounding out letters for years, started writing letters by three and a half, and has an incredible vocabulary. To me it seems he just stopped learning at the rate he was learning when I went back to work."

When Susan Feezor parlayed a volunteer position as a church administrator into a paid part-time job, she worked twenty-five hours a week and was always on hand to greet her two older children when they got home from school. Now that Susan and her husband run their own company, ExecuBusiness Centers, life as the Feezor children knew it has changed dramatically. She often works late hours. It's not surprising that her youngest, Steven, a high school junior, gives her a guilt trip because she is not there for him every day. It's been five years since the Feezors opened their business center, and her son still reminds her that she was always home for the older kids. "I make all the important activities, but I can't be supermom," she says.

Like Susan, many women find that their last child is the one who feels the brunt of Mom going back to work and is often the most vocal. It's a matter of timing. You stayed home with the older one or two, but often while the baby is still in diapers it seems to be the right time to return. Mary, who worked part-time for twelve years, was offered a full-time position with flexible hours and telecommuting when her third child was one month old. The timing was terrible, but she rationalized that such an opportunity might not come along again. She also reasoned that with two older sons and her husband, baby Colleen would get plenty of attention. The same was true for Vicki King, a lawyer on Saipan, an island about a hundred miles north of Guam in the Western Pacific, who returned to work as a legal services attorney after being at home for nine years. This mother of three said it was hardest for her youngest daughter, who was still in day care. "My daughter does complain. My husband is the one who drops her off in the morning, and he says she is fine when he does it. On the occasions I drop her off, she is very clingy. That used to make me drive the first mile away from her in tears, but it doesn't anymore."

What mother wouldn't get that wrenching feeling when her little one looks her in the eye and says, "Mom, I just like to be with you?" But as time passes, although Vicki is still conflicted, she is getting more comfortable with her decision to return to work. "I am surprised how easy it is to change gears and throw myself into work away from my children. I sometimes ruefully realize that I have become one of the mothers that I did not understand. I can rush off to a meeting leaving my slightly feverish child with a sitter, and not think of the child at all until the meeting is over. When I was home full-time, I would have found it appalling." Perhaps Vicki's guilt is assuaged because she clearly understands the reasons she went back to work. She invested a lot of time and money in her legal education and felt that with each passing year her chance of having a "meaningful" career was lessening. Her sister-in-law, who adores Vicki's daughter, was on deck to babysit and, last but certainly not least, she saw the family slipping farther into debt the longer she stayed home.

Experts tell us that the quality of the relationship is what matters; the children need to know that parents love and care about them and want what is best for them. Yet even if you reassure children and feel they are well taken care of, it's often not easy to walk out that door. Dr. Zappert calls it "driveway remorse." It's the moment you leave the house and start feeling guilty leaving your child at home. You ask yourself, "Why I am doing this? Is it worth it?" Dr. Zappert says bluntly, "Guilt comes with the territory." She suggests several strategies for lessening the guilt, including "get the facts."

When Mary went off to her part-time teaching job, her two-year-old son cried and grabbed at her leg as she went out the door. Usually she simply unclawed him and jumped into the car, ready to scream herself. But one day she had to wait for a ride and realized that she was out the door about a minute when the crying magically stopped and he started playing with the babysitter. Maybe he didn't want her to leave, but he seemingly adjusted quickly—and happily—to her being gone. It helps to remain rational and unemotional and try to answer some rudimentary questions: How long am I gone? How often am I gone? How old are the children? Am I generally reliable? Do I make promises to them that I can't keep? Do I come home when I say I will? Analyze the answers and then try to see whether your guilt is justifiable or if you are torturing yourself unnecessarily.

In Allison Pearson's novel *I Don't Know How She Does It,* a working mom bashes a pie to make it look homemade for a school bake sale so the other moms won't think it was store-bought. Where is it written that food must be made from scratch and clothes neatly pressed and beds bedecked with fancy throw pillows? Suppose you are feeling guilty because the house looks like a wrecking crew passed through. You can either wallow in the guilt or constantly yell at everyone to clean up or learn to live with it. "My mother always insisted we make beds," says Susan Feezor. "I like made beds, but in starting this business there just wasn't time. Now it doesn't bother me anymore if I leave with an unmade bed." Consider your expectations for a neat house and, even more important, if they are unrealistic. A friend passed along some words of wisdom: Everything worth doing is not worth doing well.

It's ironic, but learning to live with imperfection brings perfection to what really matters. This newfound philosophy helps you to be a better mom. Beth O'Connor said that when she worked thirty hours a week, everything in the house was not going to get done. She came to rely on a cleaning service and takeout and let go of the perfect housekeeper mind-set. That freed her to spend more time being Mom and giving the children her undivided attention. "When I am home with the kids, I am home with them.

I take them to dance lessons, storytime, have friends over. I am an at-home mom."

We come from a generation of women who have professionalized parenting. We bought the baby books and devoured them, from pregnancy through the What to Expect series. We continued with that all-encompassing attention through their school years. The problem comes when we go back to work and are no longer available at their every beck and call, which is actually a good thing. But it does take some readjustment all around. Kids who are used to Mom helping with (okay, doing) the book report at the last minute may be shocked to find that she has a dinner meeting with a client and can't help. Again, this is a good thing. Perhaps not for that book report but for the next one. Unfortunately, children, as we know too well, don't always see the big picture.

Literary agent Liza Wachter found that to be true when she went back to work full-time. Her ten- and twelve-year-old were used to Mom being available 24/7, even when she worked part-time at a bookstore. It's been an adjustment for both Liza and the children. "What I was doing before didn't impinge on our lives. I could do everything then. Now I struggle to get to all their games and to remember to buy things that they need for school. It always seems like I am a day late, and that's because there's less flexibility in my schedule."

Liza had been back at work for almost two years when we talked, and she was still trying to fine-tune the schedule. Yet, like many moms, she found that just when all seemed to be running smoothly, things started to shift out of alignment, depending on the sports season, the school schedule, her husband's work commitment, and the babysitter. Liza admitted she was loath to shift too much responsibility off her shoulders onto her husband. Her work requires constant reading, but she waits to hit the manuscripts until her children are in bed. She tries to stay off the cell when her children are in the car, but sometimes that can't be avoided during a deal-in-the-making. After our talk she sent a reflective e-mail. "I am excited about my work, and certainly they [her kids] complain about my reading so much but I am totally focused as well on my family and strive to be there for them always. When I had my third child, a friend of mine wrote to congratulate me on joining the mother-of-three club, and she wanted to let me know that it's all about who gets neglected (because with three, someone will always be neglected), not who gets the attention, and I think when you add work to this equation, it feels even more about that, but you do your best to alleviate that."

Small children usually let you know what they are thinking, whether by acting out or shouting. Teens are often harder to read. If you're going back and your children are older, they may secretly be unhappy but don't want to show it. Intellectually they understand it is your turn and perhaps that the family needs the additional income, but emotionally it's hard to let go of Mom always being there. Patricia Appleton spent more time than most moms with her three children, homeschooling them as they moved around the country for her husband's U.S. Air Force career. She even took dancing lessons with her daughters and tae kwon do with her son. About three years after she had started back to work, Pat sat with her daughters at a local Starbucks in San Antonio, Texas, relaxing after their Irish step classes. Her son joined them. Perhaps spurred by one too many lattes, the children blurted out a confession. "They started discussing how they felt 'abandoned' when I went back to work. I was shocked," says Pat.

Pat, a Korean linguist in the air force before children, had reenlisted in the reserves when her youngest turned thirteen. She was assigned to a part-time job planning training exercises, which sometimes required her to travel for a week or two. Pat had everything in place: The family lived on the base in San Antonio, and her husband came home for lunch; her daughters had part-time jobs at nearby Sea World. "The kids started having withdrawal problems," says Pat. "There was no reason this shouldn't be okay. They'd tell me 'go and go' to work and on trips but really didn't want me to. They would smile and wave good-bye because they didn't want to make me feel bad, because I had stayed home fifteen years." Ah, guilt! Would Pat have done anything differently? "I just wish they had told me about how they felt so we could discuss it."

A final suggestion from Dr. Zappert on dealing with guilt is to focus on the positive. "The proof of the rightness of our particular choices will not be apparent until our children are grown into adulthood—and then some. Given that we lack absolute proof on which to base our decision, we do have a choice. We can choose to focus on the negative—we can worry and obsess incessantly about whether we have done the wrong thing—or alternatively we can make the most informed choices possible, on the basis of the best information available." For example, instead of feeling guilty that your children are in an after-school program, focus on the enrichment, athletic, and artistic opportunities they get. Maybe you abhor arts and crafts, but every few weeks your daughter comes home with some little clay pot or charcoal drawings she made. And guess what? She knows all about how to draw using perspective. The experience is enriching; she's getting along with all kinds of children and she is learning to be responsible.

Pat's children not only survived her work and travel, they have grown into responsible young adults. One daughter, Kiyomi, now a senior anthropology major at Texas State University, volunteered in Africa one summer. The kids may turn out better than you ever dreamed. So jettison the guilt or learn to live with it, otherwise you might find yourself spending that hard-earned salary on a megabucks trip to a Florida theme park.

A DAUGHTER'S VIEW

When Pat Appleton returned to work, her teenage children encouraged her to "go, go, go." But several years later they told her the truth about how "abandoned" they really felt! In an e-mail, Kiyomi, one of the three children, explains her feelings.

Hi,

I saw nothing wrong with mothers working, and plan to be a working mom myself, but I didn't want my mom to work. It was a sudden and dramatic change. We had just moved to Texas from New England, and then went from having Mom home to almost never seeing her—literally. She returned to the Air Force and she was constantly being sent across the country or around the world.

I think a lot of it had to do with so much change at the same time. I was having culture shock—Texas is VERY different!—and then it was up to my sister and I to do most of the housework, and take on more adult roles. It seemed like my mom was off having all the fun while I was stuck home playing housewife in what was neither my home nor my family.

I can see a lot of benefits to her working now. She enjoys it, and there are certainly financial benefits. I still think the situation would have been easier on my siblings and myself if she had started working only part-time, instead of making such a sudden and complete break from the way we had been growing up.

I'm usually the spokesperson for my siblings, and we wanted her to know how we felt. After a point we began asking her to do things that wouldn't take her out of our lives completely for weeks at a time. The point of telling her we'd felt abandoned probably just came up in conversation. I appreciated that she did start to work closer to home.

I think I'll either always work, so it's something they're used to, or I'll start again only working part-time so my children have some time to get used to the idea.

The "S" Word

There's a good reason that sales of aromatherapy candles and lotions and potions are booming: stressed-out working mothers! Besides "guilt," the other word that we heard from almost every woman was "stress." While some women find stress energizing, others feel like they are being pulled at both ends like a tug-of-war rope. "Stress comes because there are only twenty-four hours in the day," says Dr. Zappert. "When you are working full-time and raising a family, even with extraordinary help, you still have stress."

Why are we so stressed? One of the primary reasons is time, as in less time. Working moms sleep less (five to six fewer hours a week), do less housework (six fewer hours), and have twelve fewer hours of free time than nonworking moms. So how do women put the brakes on before it gets out of control? Sometimes it is necessary—if finances permit—to get some extra hands in the house. For many women, hiring someone else to do the cleaning seems to be a major hurdle. Sometimes it isn't even the cost; it's admitting that you can't do it all. Getting outside help for some of the household basics also may lessen the stress between husband and wife over who does what. Keep in mind that the cost of hiring a cleaning person is far less than hiring a marriage counselor! Dawn Carlson realized this after writing her dissertation on, of all things, work-family conflict. "When I got my Ph.D., I told my husband I wasn't going to clean anymore and that we had to get someone to clean the house and mow the yard. We determined what was most important to us is how we spent our time."

In a survey of three hundred women graduates of Stanford's Business School, the number one point that working moms noted they would have done differently was "spend the money and get the help needed" and "get more help with the nonchild things." Some women willingly turn to others for help. From child care to babysitters, from relatives to friends, there is help out there. Kathryn Poling, the Defense Department lawyer, has hired a succession of au pairs. "Au pairs are like family members; they live with you and you really get to know them. We chose in-home care, again, to ease the children's transition from having Mom at home to being in care." The family's first au pair was a college junior from Lithuania, and the second was a preschool teacher from Germany. For Kathryn's younger son's birthday the au pair made the cake and muffins for his school and, together, they decorated the house. "Though I would have loved to have been there, I know the children aren't missing out," says Kathryn, coming to terms with the reality that she can't to it all. "Both my husband and I are able to be home by four P.M., so we have lots of family time."

When Linda Koch went to work at Flexible Resources, she seemingly had the ideal schedule, working three days a week from nine to three so she wouldn't need child care. But three abbreviated days a week was not enough, so she found a college student to come in three afternoons a week. All too often, just when you think you have all bases covered, schedules change and the stress-o-meter starts smoking. When Linda's son moved up to middle school, the schedule changed. "Fortunately, I have a bunch of really good friends who try to help out and I try to make it up to them. After being home for eight years and doing favors, it is difficult to adjust to the asking side."

Summertime and the Living Is Not Easy

One midsummer day we sent off an e-mail asking how the moms were doing with child-care arrangements. The replies came back fast: Summer is tough! Becky Boyd wrote, "Child care is a big pain during the summer."

No matter how organized you are and how many backups you have, summer stress hits every working mom like a wave crashing on the ocean rocks. Summers are just plain hard, not to mention expensive. With school out, so is any structure to the week. Some moms are reluctant to put kids in day care all day; with elementary school children camp sometimes fills the gap, but it's expensive and doesn't last all summer; even teens present a challenge, as one mom noted, because after the junior-counselor day-camp job there's driving to SAT prep and the travel baseball team.

When Candace Hill's kids were home for the summer, her schedule at Borders bookstore needed to be changed and child care became a problem, not to mention the added expense. "It's really difficult," agrees Linda Koch. "I've been creative; I have paid a lot more money to put them in camp. We even tried sleepaway camp. It's not easy."

Two points are clear: Flexibility is more important than ever in the summer, and strategic planning is essential. The flexibility allows you to give your children that idyllic summer you fantasize about . . . to some extent. Summer finds Staci Handschuh at the local pool club, with her children. While they go to swim team practice, Staci is parked under an umbrella writing press releases and doing the next season's budget planning and program scheduling. She says, "I am not alone. I see many moms working at the pool. A great idea would be a cybercafé at the swim club!" Staci waits until the evening to enter her work into her laptop. Yes, it requires more work, but the payoff is worth it. "I still have some flexibility with hours, but summer is a challenge. That said, I wouldn't change it for the world! I could be in a cubicle and missing this all."

If you can't get that degree of flexibility, a mélange of camps, relatives, sending the kids off to Grandma, and family vacation seems to be the way to go. Several moms hired high school or college students as summer nannies, either full-or part-time. Another mom pointed out that day camp is actually longer hours than school, so she works longer hours and then takes the time off when camp is not is session. The summer usually ends up a patchwork of this and that, and just when you have it down, the children get older and it all changes.

Worth noting: The moms who seemed to do the best had some built-in support systems in terms of relatives or friends. So think about trading off days with a neighbor for child care or sending the children to your in-laws for a week or two. Again, where you live can make a major difference. Many communities offer low-cost summer recreation and enrichment programs. The programs take care of the morning, and teenagers babysit in the afternoon. Yes, a patchwork, but if it works, why not?

While some women bring in outside help so the stress doesn't slay them, others find that having their businesses at home is the answer. Kelley Senkowski, who owns a home-based travel agency, calls it "happy stress." "It is a happy stress because I have so much. I don't have the funds yet because the commissions lag. But I don't have to worry about days the children are sick or running something to the school or vacations, and I can take off to do something with my family. I can't take off every other day, but at least I can go to the beach if I want to. I can make up work time as needed, when I choose."

These are all solutions that are mom-driven. Don't forget, though, there is help from yet another source. Yes, your children and husband.

Family Training 101: Who Will Put the Wash in the Dryer?

Fold the laundry. Check. Peel the potatoes. Check. Empty the dishwasher and walk the dog. Check. Check. This sounds like a simple to-do list for the working mom to leave for the family, but if you believe it is going to get done without some training, you're dreaming. Even if you have decided you can live with unmade beds, there are other essentials of daily life—food and water—and someone has to supply them. Cooking, cleaning, car pooling: Often new back-to-work moms try to do everything themselves, as we discovered, usually for one of three reasons. They either want to prove they can do it all, or they don't want to inconvenience the family, or they they feel, as the Carly Simon song goes, "Nobody does it better."

Like so many women returning to work, Susan Feezor, mother of three, was determined to be supermom, even though she was working long hours starting a business with her husband. "It took almost a year to realize that I can't do all this. What really brought it home was when we came home from work, Bob sat down and I was doing the cooking and laundry. This was not what I bargained for. When we started our own business, my sons and husband assumed that I would continue doing the usual 'at-home things' that I had always done. Wrong!"

It took getting through that very tough first year for Susan to realize that running her own business and a household single-handedly was impossible; she simply could not do everything she did before. Her solution was a division of labor. While Susan still does all the cooking, she hired someone to clean the house, and the kids learned how to do the laundry. "When we got to the point there were no clean clothes, I told them, 'I am working, you can do the laundry.' My husband of thirty-five years even had to figure out how to use a washer and dryer. Why didn't I have them do these things a long time ago?"

Susan's experience is typical. In our conversations with women around the country, and confirmed by our survey, we found that many moms complained that their family still expects them to do everything! Sociologist Arlie Hochschild estimated that working moms put in a full month of twenty-four-hour days over the course of a year, doing all the household chores from grocery shopping to gift buying.[2]

FROM THE GOING BACK SURVEY

Have your family's expectations of you changed since you returned to work?

44 percent: They still expect me to do the same around the house.

21 percent: They are more cooperative and pitch in more.

19 percent: Are you kidding?

16 percent: They always helped around the house.

Working moms are not getting help from the media. We may be saturated with reality TV, but where mothers and work are concerned, the portrayals are far from the truth. While more than two-thirds of "real" moms work, just one-third of TV moms work for pay.[3] Children and helping out are like two sides of a coin. One side is they want you to help them, but the other side is they don't exactly volunteer to help you! Listen in on any group of mothers—working or not—and you will hear complaints about Junior's latest leave-it-to-the-last-minute escapade where Mom was expected to come to the rescue. It's bad enough when we are at-home moms, but when working is added to the equation, the annoyance seems to divide and multiply.

It takes a strategy worthy of a corporate takeover to help children get the task done without feeling taken advantage of. We need to be "focused on the process, not just the result," says Dr. Michele

Bolton, a career consultant and author of *The Third Shift: Managing Hard Choices in Our Careers, Homes, and Lives as Women*.[4] When her eleven-year-old daughter wanted to make the traditional Purim pastry, hamantaschen, for a school celebration the same night as an eight o'clock volleyball game, Dr. Bolton realized that there would be a time crunch. If her daughter waited until after the game to start cooking, the cookie dough wouldn't be ready for baking until midnight. "I didn't see myself getting up at midnight, so I suggested using packaged cookie dough. I made half the batch to see that it came out okay. I told her she would have to make the rest. I was going to read a book and get in the hot tub. Hers weren't as good, but did I care? No! I didn't want to say, 'No, this is your problem. You should have started this earlier.' But I also didn't want to feel like a doormat, so doing half felt right." It doesn't matter whether it's pastry or a paper or pants for baseball. If children leave it to the last minute, they have to realize that it might not get done.

The other side of the coin is getting children to help more. While the learning curve may be steep, and a lot of remedial help is necessary, it is worth the effort. When Laurie Rodgers went back to school to become a teacher in her thirties, she often found herself bouncing the baby on her knee while she was writing a paper. During the first semester she tried—without success—to do everything around the house. It didn't take long for her to realize that her only hope was to enlist her two older children. "I said, 'I can't cook, clean, do laundry, do your homework and my homework. Someone is going to have to help.' We sat down and made a list of what needed to be done and what they thought they could do, from the dishes to taking out the garbage. The increased responsibility has been good for them. If you have parents who do everything, by nineteen you don't know how to boil water or do your own laundry."

Sure, there is guilt, and it hangs over you like a past-due Visa bill, but it usually mitigates as time goes by. Seeing your family fall into a routine helps. The clothes may not always be folded the way we like them, the breakfast dishes may stay piled in the sink, the mail may not be opened the same day it is delivered, but hey, some women wonder why they didn't create a division of labor years sooner. So much of our energy is devoted to making life easier for the family. Remember, it is important to put time into figuring out how to make life easier for yourself, not only the kids. Sometimes it is harder for us to adjust to the loss of control than for our families to learn the drill.

Admittedly, retraining children takes more than just giving them a to-do list. Children need some instruction, found Dr. Linda Waite, codirector of the University of Chicago's Alfred P. Sloan Center on Parents, Children and Work. The Sloan 500 Family Study surveyed two-parent families with kindergartners and teenagers to assess what works and what doesn't. One innovative aspect of the survey was that all the participants wore beeper wristwatches that rang at intervals, at which time they were required to fill out questionnaires to measure how they felt about doing a chore and how long it took to do it. The study found that the teens, for example, vastly overestimated how many hours they spent helping around the house, coming in at thirteen hours a week. The parents estimated five hours a week. The reality? Three to four hours! So when you are asking the family to pitch in, don't fall for those arguments that you're violating child-labor laws.

The study found that the most effective strategy for teaching teens is to work alongside them. Let them help you make dinner. While you grill the meat, let them stir the rice. While you iron, ask them to get the wash going. How will they know that you don't put the black pants in the washer with the whites unless you tell them? You need to be there for the instruction. "One strategy for getting kids to help is to not simply assign a task and yell at them when it's not done. Make it a joint activity and you'll find the work gets done much better when they don't feel they are doing it alone," says Dr. Waite. Interestingly, the Sloan study also found that the kids were in much better moods when they were doing housework with another family member.

In our discussions with moms, we found that as children reached middle and high school, many women made the switch to full-time jobs, on the assumption that teens needed less hands-on parenting. While teens certainly act like they don't need or want our help, just the opposite is true. The National Longitudinal Study of Adolescent Health, the largest teen study ever, involving ninety thousand adolescents, found that closeness with family was linked to less smoking, drinking, drug use, and early sex. So what are parents supposed to do?

One of the country's top experts on teens, Dr. A. Rae Simpson of MIT, analyzed more than three hundred studies on parenting adolescents in a report called "Raising Teens" for the Harvard School of Public Health. While much of her report focuses on strategies that should be used by all parents, a few findings are of particular note for working moms. The key message about parents is that they very much still matter in teenagers' lives. "Their lives are changing so frantically, from their bodies to minds to social life to educational institutions. While everything is whirlwind change, they need to know that your love is a constant," says Dr. Simpson. For example, if you're at work when they come home from school, touch base with them via e-mail or phone. "By checking in with children you are communicating that you are keeping track, not in a suspicious way but a routine way." It's also important to spend time with your teen. "Make time in whatever way you can. It may be a planned activity, or it may just be being available. The key is the availability. Make sure that a certain number of evenings you are home, because that's when teens tend to unwind."

Teens need parents, despite their protests to the contrary. Here are some guiding principles from Dr. Simpson's *Raising Teens: A Synthesis of Research and a Foundation for Action*, Project on the Parenting of Adolescents, Harvard School of Public Health[5]:

Love and Connect
- Spend time together.
- Spend time just listening.

Monitor and Observe
- Stay in touch with other parents.
- Involve yourself in school events.

Guide and Limit
- Maintain family rules.
- Communicate expectations.

Model and Consult
- Express personal positions.
- Establish or maintain traditions.

Provide and Advocate
- Network within the community.
- Make informed decisions.

Some of this is easier said than done. One mom commented that her teenager had the habit of throwing himself on the family room couch to share his worries just as she finally sat down herself to unwind at ten P.M. Dr. Simpson isn't surprised. "An example we can set for teens is to pace ourselves and have moments when we pause. If they're stressed and overwhelmed and we're not, that's very engaging and attracts them to us." For teens—as well as younger children—family traditions, whether focused on holidays or seasons or something as simple as Sunday night dinner together, are also important, notes Dr. Simpson. When Brenda Overfield started her studies to become an Episcopal priest, she also started a new tradition: Each month one son, in rotation, got a day with Mom doing whatever he wanted, even if it meant missing school. Zoos, museums, toy stores all became favorite destinations. One son still talks about the day they went to lunch at the Empire Diner in Manhattan and watched a scene from *Home Alone 2* being filmed outside.

Establishing new traditions is an excellent way to let your children see the positive side of your working, especially when it's one-on-one. From the time she started working part-time, Mary occasionally brought each child into the "big city." The deal was the child had to sit quietly in her office while Mary taught a two-hour class. The payoff was lunch at some funky restaurant and a trip to a special store or museum.

If your job comes with some perks—maybe hard-to-get baseball tickets or discount movie coupons or two seats to the taping of a TV show—make use of them. This is a not-so-subtle reminder to the family of the upside to Mom working. The same is true for a business trip. Some moms buy little presents before they go on trips so they are armed when they come home. Other moms buy T-shirts in the airport. Sometimes you don't even have to spend money. Don't turn your nose up at all the conference giveaways with company logos, from minicalculators, to CD holders, to Frisbees. What's junk to you will probably delight your ten-year-old.

TAKING A PAGE FROM FAMILY COUNSELORS, CONSIDER THESE STRATEGIES FOR GETTING EACH MEMBER OF THE FAMILY TO LIGHTEN THE LOAD

- **Start training them before you go back to work.** If Junior always helped bring the laundry down to the basement, now that he's thirteen, putting it *in* the washer should not be such a stretch.

- **Make lists.** Outline the daily, weekly, and monthly chores. Make a list for each family member. Even in the new world of Palm-Pilots, we still advise you to write on a paper calendar posted in the kitchen so everyone will see it.

- **Give your family some flexibility.** Think of this as an opportunity for your children to learn independence. Does it really matter when the dog is walked, as long as it's before he poops on the rug?

- **Give up control.** No, your daughter probably will not learn to make rice that doesn't stick, but so what? Many women want to prove that they can maintain a perfect home life even after they go back to work. From experience, we can tell you that in most cases it is not going to happen.

- **Buy in bulk.** No, we don't mean toilet tissue and paper towels at the discount warehouses. We are talking about birthday gifts and grab bag items and even holiday presents six months prior. When Mary's son was invited to a slew of sweet sixteen birthday parties, she went to a local gift shop and bought a dozen of the same gift, all store-wrapped. Over the course of the year, the gifts were ready to go. Another woman keeps a gift closet where she stashes good buys she comes across. Need a birthday gift? Out comes a present from the closet.

When the Kids Join the Team But Your Husband Is Still on the Sidelines

"My husband expects me to work eight hours, come home, cook, clean, take care of the baby, and look like a supermodel."

"My husband thinks he's a hero because he cooks dinner (about half the time) now."

Of course, a husband's life is often thrown into upheaval when his wife returns to work. Everything from money to family responsibilities to his sex life may change. One of the first sources of stress between husband and wife is the renegotiated division of family labor. The same men who ask, "Where's the ketchup?" when it is staring them in the face can't see when a simple household chore hasn't been done. You do not have to be a rocket scientist to know that the dishwasher needs to be emptied. We are not sure where the blame rests. Maybe men really are from Mars, but the simple truth is that many husbands just don't focus on what needs to be done. One mom, who obviously didn't want to be named, said, "My husband is good about his to-do list: take out the trash, empty the dishwasher, and pick up his shirts at the cleaners. But anything beyond that just doesn't seem to be on his radar unless you ask him." Another mother, in a test to prove that her family didn't help out, left a stack of neatly folded towels at the bottom of the stairs. The whole family—husband and four children—walked right past the towels for an entire week. Apparently no one thought of bringing them up to the linen closet until there wasn't a clean towel to be found upstairs.

In some ways we former stay-at-home moms have ourselves to blame because we found it easier to get the chores done on weekdays, leaving weekends free for family activities. And frankly, it still is often easier to do them ourselves. One mom, returning to work, sent her husband to the grocery store with a list. He reappeared two hours later with half the items. "You didn't specify what kind of bread," he told her. Apparently confused by the vast assortment, he didn't buy any. And what was the story with the overripe bananas? It never occurred to him not to get them if there weren't any good ones. It took several weeks of food forays before he successfully completed the shopping mission to her satisfaction. What she learned the hard way is that her husband needed some basic training. Another mom simply gave up. Her husband was supposed to comb and braid her first grader's long hair before school. The braiding was beyond him. "So now she goes to school with messy hair," the mother said, shrugging.

Without your husband's support, going back will feel more like a tidal wave than the expected rough waters. One woman who started an at-home business said her husband told her flat-out that he didn't think she could make a go of it. When he was home on an extended leave, his doubt intensified and he questioned why she was driving herself crazy. It wasn't until she landed a $1,000-a-month contract that her husband saw value in her business. It was at that point that he thought he owned bragging rights about his wife's success.

Things changed in the family household when Suellen Mazurowski returned to law school at age thirty-nine, some seventeen years after graduating from college. Suellen says that her law degree, in many ways, belongs to her children. "It was physically exhausting raising the children at the same time I was attending law school." She was fortunate in that her husband helped out. "I have learned that if you want to get men to help with the housework, you have to give them jobs they will actually do," says Suellen, who then went on to enumerate them: "Go to the grocery; barbecue on the grill; do laundry (in a pinch and do not give them things that need special care); walk dogs; run the sweeper. Do not expect them to clean in the corners. It won't happen."

Just as with children, we have to let our husbands find their way through trial and error. Dr. Barbara Waxenberg, co-coordinator of the Project in Couple and Family Therapy at New York University, remembers when her husband decided that he would take over the laundry. "I thought he was going to break both machines. I really had to sit on myself and say, 'Listen, schmuck, you weren't born knowing how to use the washer.'" Many women in our survey agreed that, after a little retraining, their husbands became more helpful and hands-on mothers' helpers. One additional benefit: Without Mom around 24/7, dads get more opportunity to establish and solidify those all-important one-on-one relationships with their children.

FROM THE GOING BACK SURVEY

Will you continue to work after your husband retires?

45 percent: Yes

55 percent: No

TURNING UP YOUR CAREER WHEN YOUR HUSBAND IS TURNING DOWN HIS

Gail Sheehy coined the term "Flaming Fifties" in her book *New Passages*[6] to describe women who become "more accepting, more outspoken, and less self-conscious." Free of home constraints and back in the workforce for a few years, these fiftysomethings may excel in their careers, becoming executives, managers, even senators. While that's great for their egos and pocketbooks, it might not be so wonderful for their husbands, who suddenly are left alone when their wives wine and dine out-of-town clients or have to work late.

Maybe your husband, now at the top of his game, wants to take three-day weekends in the summer, but it's your busy season. Or maybe he has already worked for thirty years and you are just getting started. What happens when your career is skyrocketing and he wants to call it quits? Elaine Levine's husband retired one day short of his fifty-sixth birthday. Elaine, who earned her master's degree in biology at the same time her oldest daughter was getting ready to go to college, wanted to continue working as a biologist in Monsanto's St. Louis headquarters until all three girls were through college. But ultimately she decided to retire four years after her husband. "Those four years were a struggle," says Elaine. "He was bored and lonely."

And even before he retired, Elaine and her husband, an engineering psychologist with McDonnell Douglas, were at different points in their career. "He was established, he was in his job for twenty years," says Elaine. "I don't think he was quite as stressed as I was with a new job. I would call my husband and say, 'The bacteria grew slowly so I am not coming home until they grow.'

On occasion, I didn't get home until eleven or twelve at night. All I wanted to do was just collapse."

There is no doubt about it; Elaine felt guilty. She felt guilty that her husband was doing more than he signed on for, like starting dinner because he was home by four. She felt guilty that she was not always a cheery wife, although she certainly never stopped trying. "The perfect marriage is where each partner gives 75 percent," says Elaine. "I won't go that far, but more than 50 is what worked for me."

NYU's Barbara Waxenberg says that when a husband retires and his wife still works, it creates a disparity in power. The husband slows down, mentally and physically, yet the wife scurries around like the Energizer Bunny. While the husband is looking forward to the golf course, his wife, who returned to work, is just hitting her stride and relishing her business achievements. In terms of vim and vigor, there's often a difference too. Women tend to be younger than their spouses, and considering the survival statistics, in better health. Dr. Waxenberg urges couples to understand each other's needs by communicating. "When a man retires, unless he has a huge pension, his resources have diminished, and, especially if a woman is successful, the power balance goes where money is," she says. She believes that psychological warfare can erupt during times of transition, and it becomes most important to watch for warning signs.

For husbands, our returning to work can be a double whammy. Besides your not always being there for him, your husband may see a new you. After years of running around in sweats and sneakers, many women begin dressing for the office and schmoozing with men who aren't soccer coaches. From Weightwatchers to Atkins, from Pilates to a personal trainer, many women get new bodies for the new job. So don't be surprised if signs of jealousy surface. "It's an issue that should be worked out," says marriage and career counselor Naomi Resnik. "While it may have raised these women's self-esteem, their husbands are thinking, 'I didn't expect her to look so good, but I am glad she lost the weight. I don't want her interacting with other men looking like that.' It goes to how strong the relationship is."

Naomi suggests six coping strategies to help your marriage survive the stresses and strains of returning to work.

- **Seek professional help.** Instead of this being the final resort, put it at the top of your list. Don't wait until it's too late.
- **Have a support network in place.** This network is different for every woman. Some look to family members; others turn to their mentors or friends.
- **Keep the lines of communication open.** Each member of the family has a role, a job, a personality. A change in the dynamics, like Mom returning to work, causes a shift in what Naomi calls the "family mobile." When the winds of the workforce blow, it is important that the lines of communication remain open.
- **Use creative planning.** Loosen those reins and delegate, delegate, delegate. There is no getting around it; your husband is going to have to assume some responsibility that he didn't have before. "Some men have been spoiled," says Naomi. "From car pooling to one-on-one time with the children, he has to help out in some way."

- **Learn relaxation techniques.** Taking a deep breath works well. Naomi has her patients do deep-breathing exercises to relax. Using the Subjective Units of Discomfort scale (SUDS), Naomi determines the couple's level of discomfort on a scale from 1 to 100. "If they are screaming, their SUDS level is above 30. We do relaxation techniques to get the SUDS level down below a 30, and then their communication will be more productive."
- **Role-play.** In couples counseling, Naomi likes spouses to switch seats, trying to make each of them understand how the other feels. "Role-playing and switching allows you to zoom in on your feelings rather than escaping to your brain."

Your Sex Life: You Thought You Were Tired Before

Remember those first years of parenthood? Sex may not have been high on your to-do list. The same with the pressures of a new job. The days or weeks can run into one another, but you and your husband may not. In a recent survey of twenty-one hundred mothers nationwide, *Redbook* magazine found that full-time working moms had sex less than once a week, compared to at-home moms, who were likely to have sex two to three times a week. And it's not only sex. Just time to sit down together and connect on a conversational level seems to vanish.

In spite of these numbers, many women are not overly worried about the lack of couple time when Mom goes back to work. "Neither Dan nor I seem terribly concerned about less time to-gether," says attorney Kathryn Poling. "Part of it is that we are just practical people and know that this period with our children will end in a blink. Part of it is that we married older and had very separate lives to begin with. But the real bottom line is that since we both have good jobs with reasonable hours, we feel like we do have time together."

When Loretta spoke to a new mothers' group in New York City, it was only a matter of minutes before the conversation went from nursing to sex. These women, many of them professionals, had given up a lot to be at-home moms—fast-track careers and big salaries—but they made it blatantly clear that they were not going to give up sex. One woman said that once a week she hired a babysitter, said goodnight to her toddler who was usually watching a video, left, and then unlocked the door to return with her husband to their bedroom. Sounds bizarre? Don't knock it until you try it.

HOW TO KEEP THOSE HOME FIRES FLAMING

- Makes dates with your husband. Plans always bring with them an anticipatory excitement.
- Check out women's magazines. They always have recommendations for improved relations (and positions).
- If you are zonked every night, consider morning sex instead of a jog. Start charting sex on your personal calendar, not the kitchen calendar that lists everyone's responsibilities!
- Remember those days of taking your temperature to chart your ovulation? Mark your calendar when you have sex to make sure that you have not put it too far down on your to-do list.
- If all else fails, take your husband on one of your business trips.

What About Me?

Forget lunch with the girls and the monthly book club. The reality is that even if the family pitches in and you find extra hands to help with cleaning or mowing the lawn, you may have to ditch your own extracurricular activities. Vicki King says there is just no time. There were so many things she enjoyed doing, from gardening to writing letters to the editor to mentoring teen moms, that can't find their way back into her busy day. "I do miss setting my own schedule and my own priorities," she says. "But my day at work goes by in a busy fulfilling whirl and then it's time to pick up the kids and take them to swimming, music lessons, do homework, etc. The other day I was wondering to myself, 'Why don't I garden anymore?' Duh, I have a job now, and I just don't have the time for extra things."

Mary understands exactly what Vicki means. Ask her if she had a busy social life after she went back to teaching, and her answer is a flat-out no. She understood that this was the sacrifice she had to make as a working mom. "I had family and work but not much time for anything else. I even gave up the PTA when the meetings fell on workdays. I couldn't see being at work all day and then going out at night." Mary would love to spend more time schmoozing with her colleagues, but it just isn't possible. When she is at NYU, she has to use her time there for classes, counseling students, or hiring adjuncts. After continually turning down a colleague who invited her to lunch, the woman finally asked, "Well, when *can* you go out to lunch?" Mary's reply: "When I am fifty and my children are older." "You'll be boring by then," her colleague replied. The good news, as any mom knows, is that children grow and leave the house (or prefer not to be seen with you), and life does change. You will get time again for your own pleasurable pursuits, and you'll be too busy to be boring at fifty!

If you have young children underfoot, there are ways not to give up your entire social life, says Dr. Dawn Carlson, coauthor of *Beyond Juggling*.[7] She suggests "bundling," the mother of multitasking, where you tie together a number of activities into one neat package. "When you work and have kids, you don't have time for friends," says Dr. Carlson, a Baylor University professor and a thirty-five-year-old mother of toddler twins and a preschooler. She explained how she "bundled" when she and her children recently gathered at a friend's house to make spice tea mix that the children and moms then brought to a local senior citizens' home. "If I can do a church service project with some friends plus the kids, it was socializing and also doing something for the church," she says, noting that an added benefit was a time for mom talk. "Some women who don't work do playgroups, and while the kids are playing they can discuss potty training or whatever. I can't go to playgroups and, trust me, the guys who I work with don't care about it."

If your time is limited but you can squeeze in one or two extracurriculars, how to choose? Dr. Bolton tells the clients she counsels that they should come up with three things that they are not willing to sacrifice. "I always loved the 'Rule of Three,'" she says. "We must be willing to compromise, but we must distinguish between what feels like a compromise or a sacrifice. For example, for me it's a compromise that I don't see every one of my son's home baseball games, but I am not willing to sacrifice the most important game of the season for an appointment."

One woman will not give up exercising. On occasion, she may have to reschedule the time she exercises, but in no way is she x-ing it off her schedule. Another woman is not willing to miss her monthly luncheon with her college roommates. Or maybe you cannot go without reading the newspaper with your morning coffee. Or maybe you just won't give up a weekly manicure. Okay. You will settle for every two weeks, but that's it!

Some women told us that they sometimes second-guess the choices they made, wondering how life would be different if they had not back-burnered their careers or if they'd had a third child. Our advice: Stop worrying about the past and choices you didn't make. Instead focus on the present and the future, and start exploring the different choices that are open to you now. If your routine does not seem to be working for you, even though it might be fine for your husband and children, then think about changing it . . . again. Some of the most successful women, in terms of balancing work and family, admit that they often rejigger their schedules. Dr. Bolton decided to start taking Fridays off. "Just taking one day off increased my weekend by 50 percent and I realized it's like a miracle. I will never wear out at this pace and I will keep on ticking and working."

When You Become Your Mom's Mom

If you come away from this book with one indelible idea, it should be that you need to plan your comeback, not unlike a fighter returning to the ring. But here comes the bad news: You may be working toward your return, or you may have just gone back, when you find that you have to take a leave to care for an ailing parent. Surprisingly, even younger returnees may have to face this scenario. When the National Partnership for Women and Families asked thirtysomethings how likely is it that they would be responsible for the care of an elderly parent or relative, 31 percent said it was very likely and 54 percent said it was somewhat likely.[8]

Sheila Ballard actually sent out cold résumés and got job offers within two weeks, but turned them down because she felt responsible for helping to care for her aging parents. From grocery shopping to cleaning to banking, she makes herself available to help her parents, but she finds it leaves little time to pursue a new career. What's more, she helps out her husband's mother, who is partially paralyzed from a stroke she suffered in her forties. "My parents depend on me and my Marine Corps brother because we are the take-charge siblings who have exhibited the most consistency out of the five and therefore are more depended upon," says Sheila.

Taking care of her parents, her mother-in-law, and her four-year-old son makes it difficult for Sheila to charge into a new career. Instead, this former auto claims adjuster took a job as a field inventory rep for car dealerships. She makes the rounds of eight dealerships and creates a list of the available used cars for sale. "Right now I took a part-time, no-brainer job," says Sheila. "It gives me something to do and it gives me a few dollars in my pocket. I am pretty happy, but at times I want to do more for myself. I have friends who work, and at times they make you feel that you're not doing enough because you stay home."

It sounds as if her friends don't know how busy Sheila really is. Her husband started a real estate business, buying houses, renovating them, and then renting them out. Owning twelve homes, Sheila shows the houses, maintains the properties, meets with contractors, pays the bills, and invoices the tenants. Although she is not working in broadcast administration, the field in which she received her master's degree from Norfolk State University, she says that her husband reminds her that a lot of people would like to be in her shoes.

Right now, Sheila is not thinking about a future career, although one friend is trying to convince her to become a teacher and another is urging her to get a master's in nursing. For now, with her four-year-old Sam at home, three parents who need her attention, and an array of other responsibilities, an entirely new career is on the back burner.

How Can Married Children Still Need a Mommy?

Women who are going back when their children are grown face unique issues ranging from the economic to the emotional. Struggling thirtysomethings see Mom and Dad making a nice living and taking an exciting European vacation . . . for the first time. When they not-so-subtly ask, "How about helping out with a down payment for a house?" it gives you pause. You had other plans for your salary. Or when the holidays roll around and your family feels betrayed if you don't whip up your usual better-than-Martha meal. What's a mother to do?

For some women, the part-time or flexible or telecommuting job they went back to, which worked well with mothering, also goes great with grandmothering. Sue Wechsler, a psychologist from Chevy Chase, Maryland, believes that. "My daughter has grandma plans for me," says Sue. "But I am fortunate to have a profession that I can cut back."

For those of you who aren't grandparents yet, this scenario might be hard to imagine. For those women who are and help care for grandchildren, these are very real issues. You've told your daughter since the time she was a tot, "You can have it all." She has decided to return to work and wants you—a recent returnee as well—to babysit. Talk about being torn. Nothing gives you more pleasure than spending time with the grandkids. But, and there is a but here, you have launched a new work life that comes with re-sponsibility and commitments. It may hurt to say it, but now is the time to invoke yet another eighties slogan: "Just Say No." And this may also be the time to teach your daughter two new words: Day care.

Fearing an onslaught of e-mails from new grandmas, we have to say that we spoke with many working women who happily volunteer to care for their grandchildren. Some of these career women have reworked their schedules so that one day a week is dedicated to grandmothering. All of these women expressed the same sentiment about having grandchildren: "It's indescribable." All of them say that the time they spend with their grandchildren is gratifying and fulfilling and beyond imagination. Ask Phyllis Segal, a Boston lawyer with a full plate. Besides serving as the chair of the Brady Center to Prevent Gun Violence, she has a consulting and mediation practice and also teaches negotiation. Still, when Wednesday rolls around, you can find Phyllis smiling from ear to ear, looking forward to spending the day with her two grandchildren. "Because I am there for a limited time I am able to focus on just being with them, as I often couldn't with my own children," she explains. "I am not distracted by other things I need to get done because I know I can do them later. For me, being with the grandbabies is a pure joy."

We do learn from our mothers, and Phyllis's mother was her role model. "My parents were there for me and my children and let me follow my professional pursuits. That gave me the comfort and safety to work. Because of my investment in career throughout the past decades, I am now able to compose a professional life in which I structure my own time and not let work get in the way of spending a precious day with my grandchildren."

Can Your Family Help You Be a Better Worker?

We certainly know that work and family can conflict, and this whole chapter is devoted to minimizing the conflict. But what about mutual enhancement? If you're happy at work, can that help your home life, and vice versa? Academic experts are just beginning to study this area, and they've dubbed it "facilitation and enhancement," according to Dr. Carlson. Some benefits are so basic that we often don't even acknowledge them. Communication skills that you use with your children and husband can be effectively translated to the workplace to help get your message across to a coworker who (like your family members) may not always be listening. The time management techniques you use at work can help you get through the ever-growing to-do list at home. "It can go both ways in that family enhances work and vice versa. We're just not sure which impacts which more," says Dr. Carlson.

Six

Workplace Culture Shock

I work harder than anyone in my office. Maybe part of it's that I'm just trying to prove myself, but I think part is that the work ethic among younger people just isn't what it used to be. The whole office—in clothes and attitude—has gone casual.

—fortysomething corporate executive

I don't think the workplace has changed so much since I left as much as my view of work and how I perform has changed—my life doesn't revolve around my work and the office. I still strive to do a good job but it isn't a live-or-die situation any longer.

—survey response

RETURNING TO THE OFFICE can be a culture and computer shock. The staff is padding around in mules and tank tops, plugging in PalmPilots to laptops. Your boss, barely out of his twenties, brings his dog to the office but heaven forbid you bring your kid when the babysitter doesn't show. What happened in the five or more years you were away? The workplace has certainly changed! The question is: Can you adjust?

Let's start with the basics. Women from the Gloria Steinem sisterhood may not like hearing this, but look in the mirror. Your back-to-work image is important. It is the first way people judge you, like it or not. You don't have to sport stilettos or have your pants hanging below your belly button. But you should not look like you were locked up for the past few years or, worse, for the last decade. "Pay particular attention to how you look. Try not to wear the same hairstyle that dates you. This might be a terrible thing to say, but look at me," says Professor Phyllis Moen of the University of Minnesota, who abandoned the gray grandma look for a spiky, I-know-what's-hip, highlighted hairdo.

Before going on your job interview, do your homework, do some investigative reporting. Are you headed to a coat-and-tie kind of company, or is it an anything-goes workplace? This is not to suggest that if flip-flops are the footwear of choice for the twentysomething employees, you should run out to buy them. But you may want to leave your panty hose and pumps at home and opt for a sweater set and pants. When we met Phyllis Moen in late fall we could not help thinking that this is a woman who knows what to wear, when and how, looking chic yet appropriate at the Cornell Club in midtown Manhattan. Amid Federal furniture and faux fallen leaves on the fireplace, on a crisp October morning, Phyllis was wearing brown slacks and a pumpkin-colored sweater, with a cheerful coordinating chiffon scarf loosely tied around her neck.

Be open to new ideas about your personal image. When Mona Behan went to work at The Dr. Spock Company, she took the lead from her coworkers but had to put her own spin on what she wore to work. "What I got was tons of advice on my clothes. I dressed very conservatively. I would watch and see them wear simpler and tighter clothes. I can't do too much of that, but I tried. I went from Brooks Brothers to Inc."

FROM THE GOING BACK SURVEY

Since returning to work, how do you feel about yourself?

24 percent: Proud of my success

23 percent: More stressed

22 percent: Conflicted

16 percent: Happier

14 percent: Less bored

Other comments:

On the upside: glad to get out of the house; like I am getting a second education; more balanced; more financially secure; valuable; reconnected with my professional self

On the downside: bad mommy; sad; sleepy; miss taking care of my family full-time; miss helping out at school

Getting Lost on the Information Superhighway

So you go to your first day at work confident that you look cool, calm, and collected. That is until you sit down at your desk and switch on the computer and are greeted with dozens of e-mails. Some spam, some questions demanding immediate responses, and some pointing you to Web sites with important information that you should scan before the end of the day. The message light on your phone blinks furiously. *Beep, beep!* Now it's your Black-Berry (which you really don't know how to use yet) indicating "a meeting is taking place RIGHT NOW" in the conference room. You grab your carryall to pull out your presentation and realize that you have Susie's third-grade book report instead. Welcome to the information superhighway. How will you ever get on? Are you doomed to the slow lane?

Even if you have been away from the office only a few years, you'll find some big changes. One of the most startling is the furious flow of information that comes at you online, in person, and on paper. Even multitasking marvels can be daunted. Not only are you expected to devour enormous amounts of information but you're also supposed to access it online within seconds. In the three years Defense Department lawyer Kathryn Poling was home, legal research went digital. "When I left, all my work was in books and a little online. Now everything is available online. I had to learn how to find Web sites for everything, and no one ever says, 'Go to http whatever.' They just tell you it's on the Web and you have to find it!"

William Warren, executive director of the E-Recruiting Association, agrees that the flow of information has accelerated in the last few years. "We have seen it quite often with people who had worked for us in the past and come back. We have been surprised they haven't kept up. Knowing how to handle the information overload is very critical for success."

Strategies for dealing with information overload range from working seventy hours a week to downloading to a laptop that goes everywhere with you. (Oops! Junior just hit a home run. Missed it!) If these solutions are not appealing, here are some other tactics we suggest. First, don't wait until you go back to work to learn how to surf the Web. Get some driving lessons on the information superhighway. While adult ed classes are good, we like the one-on-one approach with a nerdy high school student. As least you won't feel stupid asking dumb questions. The key here is practice, practice, practice so on the first day back to work you'll feel at ease managing information from the Internet.

Second, learn time-saving techniques. You can spend hours on the Internet looking for information if you don't know how to search. Google is just the first step, not the last stop. Check out your library or local Y for research classes. Be brave; venture beyond your comfy service provider and into the hidden world of government documents and organization home pages. Start by finding several Web sites related to your work and follow the links wherever they take you. They will give you a clue as to what others in your industry are reading. Bookmark a set of pages to check weekly, if not daily, so you don't miss out on important developments. Limit your aimless surfing. You can waste hours on the Web. If you want to browse, set aside some time, as you might for a magazine or TV show, and surf aimlessly for thirty minutes and then click off.

Don't feel that you must read everything. There's just no way you can keep up with every relevant site on the Web. Learn to be ruthless and fast-forward through what is interesting but not essential to your work. The same goes for e-mail. While it is tempting to answer e-mail the minute it comes in, to survive you must learn to compartmentalize it to three or four times a day. Mary, who gets dozens of daily e-mails, used to answer them immediately. But that didn't give her blocks of time to work on other projects. When she replied immediately, invariably another response came right back and she found herself in a game of cyberspace ping-pong. Remember, if you set up expectations with people that you are an instant replier, they come to want that level of attention all the time. That's what Mary Burich found when she went back to work as manager of internal communications for Delaware North Companies. Her company manages food, hospitality, and recreation services at locations from the Kennedy Space Center to Yosemite National Park, so she is deluged with e-mails at all hours. "I am a sitting duck for trying to answer them immediately. I hate loose ends and like everything tidy, so I feel compelled to answer all the phone and e-mail messages. I am sitting here and the message light blinks and the e-mail alarm goes off and it's hard not to get distracted." When she needs a block of uninterrupted time, she uses a couple of techniques to help her manage, from turning off the e-mail beeper to working at home without the distractions of the office. One of our colleagues reads and answers e-mail early morning, midafternoon, and late evening. That's it: three times a day! Difficult but a great time saver.

E-mail and Internet surfing are not the only high-tech tricks you are supposed to know. Mona Behan taught herself how to speed along the information superhighway during her years of freelance writing and editing. So when she went back to a full-time job at a dot-com she was confident she could handle the work. But they didn't expect her only to know how to edit copy submitted by doctors and other experts, she was also supposed to know some HTML coding for Web pages. "At the first meeting I went to I felt like people were speaking a different language. I kept my mouth shut and turned to my boss at the meeting and said, 'They are not speaking my language.' He turned to me and said, 'This is your language now.'"

For Mona, it was like a cram course at Berlitz. Highly motivated, she caught on very fast. "At first, I was the only editor and I had to do hundreds and hundreds of articles," says Mona. "I learned enough HTML to get by and to put an article on a computer template. I had to learn a new style of editing. Thankfully, the Web is very forgiving, so if you make a mistake you can fix it, unlike it being in print. It was baptism by fire."

A further effect of high-speed technology: It has raised the bar on how much work we can be expected to manage. That was the major change that Mary Burich found when she returned to the corporate world after five years at home. "We're conditioned to do more work faster simply because it can be done thanks to everything from cell phones to e-mail. Also, because of the downturn in the economy, we're doing more work with less resources." As a result of the more-faster-now mentality, many women find it hard to turn it off when they get home. The impulse is to check e-mail, phone messages, the pager the minute you walk in the door. We think that if we can just answer those last few e-mails that popped up while we were commuting we'll put the lid on the work for a while. But in a global economy, that simply doesn't happen. If you want to be there for your family when you are home, you must truly be there. You may go through withdrawal, but when you leave the office—at whatever time—if you possibly can, call it a night, or at least until the kids are in bed. Several women we know get up extra-early to check their e-mail and phone messages before they go off to work. And an e-mail at six A.M. seems a lot more efficient and organized than one composed as an afterthought at ten P.M. Would you believe that business owner Carolyn Minerich, who gets to work by six-thirty every morning, dismantled her home office and even got rid of her home computer? "I work very hard at work, but I have to take time off from work at home."

Don't be afraid to set boundaries where work ends and home begins. Many times women are their own worst enemies, feeling a constant need to prove themselves. They hired you; if you gave them 100 percent during work hours, then it's okay to leave the office behind, both literally and figuratively.

THE NEWFANGLED WORKPLACE: WAS I REALLY AWAY TOO LONG?

While the change in technology might be the most monumental, you will come face-to-face with other workplace changes. This list may help you avoid the initial-shock gasps or, worse, fainting.

- **Co-ed bathrooms.** If you thought there was a unisex only in Ally McBeal's fictitious law firm, you're wrong. Even Mary has a co-ed restroom at NYU.
- **Self-evaluations.** You may have been used to annual reviews by your boss, not writing your own report card. Don't be surprised when a four-page questionnaire is on your e-mail or in your mailbox asking you to rate—on a scale of 1 to 10—your contribution to the company.
- **Fewer face-to-face meetings.** If you think that it's your facial expressions or body language that gives you an edge at a strategy meeting or a negotiation, forget it. Today's meetings are conference calls or back-and-forth e-mails, leaving little room for old-world strategy.

How to Succeed in Business by *Really* Trying

While technology may be the most visible reminder of how the workplace has changed, there's another equally startling change: Look into the cubicle next to you. Your coworker is a Gen Xer, one of those babies born between 1963 and 1982 who grew up in a work world of layoffs, long hours, and leaner, meaner business. These workers are not hanging around to get the gold watch celebrating twenty-five years of service or looking toward a nice pension at the end of forty years with the same company. The reality is that the era of the company man and woman is long over and, as a result, Gen Xers' attitude toward work may be very different from yours.

Bruce Tulgan, founder of RainmakerThinking, Inc., a management-training firm known for its research on young workers, explains, "The old idea was that you must pay dues to climb the ladder and that seniority mattered. Gen Xers don't feel that way. They started their careers in the midst of a workplace revolution, in which the employer-employee relationship has changed forever. And the big difference with Gen Xers, and Gen Yers too, is that they have never known it any other way. They see themselves as free agents not company people." As the leading edge of Gen X turns forty and increasingly moves into management positions, they will write the rules of office politics. If you want to get in the game, it helps to know the new rules. "Recalibrate your expectations and take a new approach to your career," Mr. Tulgan advises. "Try to accept changes in the business world and reorient your own career mind so that you see you're in business for yourself and you need to take responsibility for your own learning."

So how exactly do you do that? How do you compete with the young kids? These "kids" from Gen X—and soon Gen Y—will be your colleagues and maybe even your bosses. It is critical that you play the game on their fields. In fact, many businesses use the team approach. You want to get yourself on the best teams, the ones that get the plum assignments. To avoid this becoming the grown-up version of the gym nightmare where you're the last person picked for a team, you must learn to identify what your value is to the company. What can you do best—or at least better than anyone else? In what way can you make yourself indispensable? "Remember, the number one thing to do with colleagues of all ages, but especially younger ones, is to be seen as immensely valuable," says Mr. Tulgan. "You need to become the go-to person on something. You're the person who always meets or beats deadlines. In a nutshell, you can be counted on to do work very well and very fast, and you're the person everyone wants on their project."

When Loretta started out as a freelance journalist, she often filed her stories before the deadline. Without exception, each and every time she called the editor to say that the article was ready, there was gleeful surprise at the other end of the phone. "It's done?" or "But it's not due until next week," or "Writers usually ask for extensions," were the usual replies. Loretta is convinced that her old-world work ethic was one of the reasons that so many editors gave her repeat assignments. She was low maintenance. She got the assignment, got it done, and she never missed a deadline. In the publishing world, that's worth a lot.

Don't panic. No one is asking you to run the company with one hand tied behind your back. You simply need to identify some project or task that you can do and be counted on to perform—

par excellence. When Mary first began teaching at NYU, there was a course on magazine editing that the department chair had trouble filling each semester. Mary got herself up to speed on the topic and for ten years taught it semester after semester. She gradually became the go-to person for a variety of different projects that the department needed done. Sometimes they were not exactly glamorous, but they all added up when it came time to apply for a full-time position. A side note: The best thing that ever happened in that magazine class is that she met a returning graduate student—Loretta!

Managers, no matter what their age, want to know they can delegate an assignment and it will be done the right way, the first time. We have found over and over that mothers seem particularly adept at this, perhaps because as managers of their own households they face similar challenges. Whatever the reason, they have the ability to focus and get the job done expertly. "Your job as a worker is to convince the employer that you are going to add value, you are going to make them look good," says Monique LaCour, owner of Career Management Services in Houston, Texas. "The better you make the boss look, the longer you stay in your job. I have had three-month contracts extended into a year because of that."

Don't be shy about advertising your accomplishments. Obviously we don't mean an in-your-face, look-what-I-did approach. But too many returning women are willing to sit back and let others bask in the glory. Again, learn a lesson from Gen X and take credit for your accomplishments and let the powers that be know what you contributed.

While you might not have a lot of downtime to investigate new projects at work, you must always keep on the lookout for the next good opportunity. Again, don't hesitate to be put on that project. The whole mind-set of Gen X is, "What are you going to do for me?" Remember, they see themselves as free agents, trying to get the best deal they can from the highest bidder. If you expect to compete successfully with them, you need to change your way of thinking. The payoff in the new world of work is that you, in turn, can expect a return from your employer. "You must also start to think in terms of getting your own needs met in that you can't expect someone else to take care of you," says Bruce Tulgan. "No one is going to come along and say 'Gee, do you need a flexible schedule?'"

FROM THE GOING BACK SURVEY

What is the best part about going back to work?

34 percent: Money

23 percent: Sense of achievement

20 percent: Sense of self-esteem

13 percent: Office camaraderie

8 percent: Time alone while commuting

2 percent: Lunch

Comments: adult conversation; fulfillment; learning new skills; using my brain; meeting new people; pursuing a passion; helping others; doing something that is good for my soul

---

How Can I Call Him "Mister" When My Boss Is Half My Age?

If you can't, don't go there. It's the way of the world. Dealing with a younger boss is really a metaphor for dealing with a work attitude that has changed radically since Gen X entered the workforce. And watch out, here comes Gen Y (born after 1980) already notorious for an unwillingness to perform menial tasks that they probably did during one of their many college internships.

This may be hard to swallow, but for some of you, your youngest coworkers may be the same age as your children. How exactly do you relate to these people? Like a contemporary? Like a mom? Start doubling up on your gym workouts? And what happens when you want to plow through the workload so you can get out the door at a decent hour and they want to "hang" for a while?

Just ask Mona about her cohorts at The Dr. Spock Company. "Most of my coworkers were much younger than me. Case in point: One new coworker asked, 'When did you graduate college?' I thought about lying, but I am so bad at math that I couldn't subtract the years fast enough. So I told her the truth, that I graduated college in 1976, and she said, 'That was the year I was born!' I hated her," Mona says with an affectionate laugh.

"Once I got over the age difference, we all got along. I was the cool mom who didn't pass judgment on them, and we did have so much in common. We discussed everything from relationships to careers. I was not seen as someone who was ambitious, playing the political part. I had lot of experience at IBM and *Parenting* magazine, and in a lot of different realms. I have been there, done that."

The approach that worked for Mona can work for you too. Stay away from the holier-than-thou attitude and instead share your experiences as just that, experiences, not hard-and-fast rules to be followed. Mary often finds when she gives graduate students reporting assignments that there are always a few Lone Rangers who want to try it their way rather than follow her advice, which is based on years of experience. So she lets them do it their way; sometimes they surprise her and she learns something new. Most times the assignment doesn't pan out, and the next time the students learn to heed her guidance. The same is true in the work world: Make suggestions but don't come across as Ms. Schoolmarm.

When you left work, perhaps you were one of the younger staffers. Now you feel as though your age is tattooed on your forehead and people are pointing fingers. When Susan Seigel started a new career as a fortysomething student teacher, one of the pupils raised her hand and said, "I talked to my father about you. My father told me that student teachers are supposed to be young." Sure, some are, but Susan believes that being older and a mom worked in her favor. "I was more mature and had a lot less discipline problems because the kids know 'she is a mommy person.'"

Sometimes even a thirtysomething can feel out of the loop. It's hard to decide whether you just seem old to the twentysomething staff (horrors!) or missed changes even in a few years away from the office. Social worker Karen Shriver went to work at a West Virginia youth advocate program, doing home studies and meeting with men and women who wanted to become foster parents. She was out of the workforce for only three years, but she certainly saw changes when she returned. She got the feeling that her coworkers thought it would be disrespectful or rude to take her on. "We would be discussing a case and I'd say, 'Maybe we should do this.' They didn't say maybe we should or maybe we shouldn't. They just looked down. It was almost like they were saying, 'We respect our elders.'" So don't go back expecting to hear your younger coworkers say that your opinion is important because "you're more experienced." It's just not going to happen. In fact, you might be the only one at the meeting who believes that your age—be it thirty or fifty—brings wisdom to the table.

What Karen realized is that, yes, she was more experienced, but many things had changed during her years at home, from laws governing foster families, to regulations about fire drills, to babysitter guidelines. Karen admits that she didn't keep up with the changes while she was at home with her two children. "The new laws just pop up in day-to-day conversation. It's like I lived in a shell for three years."

Not everyone can handle working with or for someone who is so much younger. One woman told us that the thing she hated most about her job was working for a Gen-X boss who is "as green as they come and as young as they come. I can teach him how to blow his nose." And the feeling may be mutual, says Connie Fuller, coauthor of *Bridging the Boomer Xer Gap*.[1] "The boss's concern about the boomer is that she won't be flexible enough and is not open to doing new things and perhaps is locked into a narrow role." So how do you prove him or her wrong? "Find a niche and find a job that no one else will be willing to do. Be open-minded and go where you are needed and create an expertise," says Dr. Fuller.

But if you are just going back, how do you find a niche? Dr. Fuller suggests that you start reading the want ads regularly even before looking for a job. "The want ads tell where the demand is for what kinds of work. You must pay attention to your job category and watch for what kind of expertise employers want." As an example she pointed out that in the human resources field there has been an increasing demand for compensation specialists. Of course, reading business and trade publications is also another way to find out where a particular industry is heading.

Now let's switch hats for a minute. Suppose you are not working for a younger boss. Rather, you are the boss and find yourself managing Gen X and Y. That may require a recalibration of the management style you used BC. As much as you might like to send a younger employee to a time-out chair for misbehavior, that strategy won't work. Bruce Tulgan advises that with younger workers, the key is to link accountability directly with flexibility. Some of Mary's former graduate students stay in touch with her, and their big complaint is that their work is not challenging enough. "I did all this as an intern," is a common lament. However, they don't mind sixty-hour weeks if occasionally there are some tradeoffs in time. Flexibility knows no age bounds. Sometimes these Gen-Y workers are surprised that their bosses don't immediately see the wisdom of their suggestions and can't understand why their ideas are not implemented. While Gen X has been slapped with the slacker stereotype, Gen Y is just the opposite: They expect to work hard and they expect rewards . . . now. And watch your back because some of them feel they can do your job better.

The best way to manage Gen X and Y, according to Bruce Tulgan and other experts, is to provide challenging work with clear goals and deadlines. Remember, you may be the boss, but you're all on the same team (and that team occasionally likes to get treated to lunch). Provide feedback and try to find something positive to say. At NYU, the number-one complaint that Mary hears about professors is that they don't give enough constructive criticism on papers. As one professor advised another, "Try to start with something good in your comments, even if its 'nice typeface.'" Finally, be respectful. The Golden Rule, "Do unto others as you would have them do unto you," applies even in the office. If you treat coworkers with respect, it is likely you will get the same back.

Social Life: Drinks with the Office Gang or Pizza with the Kids?

Both are important. You don't have to be like Ally McBeal and go to the bar every night, but a once-in-a-while birthday celebration with a coworker is just fine. Mona Behan and her friend from work, Rachel, flew to Gloucester, Massachusetts, for the wedding of their coworker, age thirty. "I worked with a very talented pool of fun, invigorating people, and it definitely widened my circle of friends. We went hiking, took in plays and movies, and went out for dinner. They even turned me on to one of Hemingway's favorite drinks, mojitos. On Friday nights, we would often get together at my house for garlic pizza and mojitos and rent videos." Susan Seigel may not have the high school faculty over for mojitos, but her colleagues like to share stories about their love life with her. Since Susan's daughter is the same age as many of the new hires, there is often common ground for discussion.

Susan Feezor, who manages a business center in North Carolina, has several employees in their twenties, the same ages as her children. She makes the staff feel comfortable, valued, and like an office family. "Sometimes it is really hard not to be their mom, but I have learned to not offer advice unless asked. We talk about movies, politics, fashion trends, cooking, religion, and how much things have changed since I was their age. They really think it is funny when I know the words to a 'new song' that is really a remake of song from years ago. We all like Aerosmith, the Beatles, Eric Clapton, Sting, the Dave Matthews Band, and the Rolling Stones, but I also like Alan Jackson, Tim McGraw, and Brooks and Dunn. That is hard for them to understand. Occasionally I get the rolling of the eyes, but basically we all get along well together."

Susan knows that the key ingredient to working with a staff of any age is to make them feel valued and appreciated, so twice a month she supplies lunch. While munching away, the staffers talk about business, how they feel about work, and what can be done to make things better for them and their clients. Lunch venting works; Susan has happy employees. "When Emily's father had a heart attack eighteen months ago, she was very surprised when we insisted she take off time and go stay with him in Wisconsin while he recovered. After her return, she kept thanking us for giving her time off. She said it made her feel good that we actually cared about her as a person, not just as an employee. We are the same age as her parents, but she considers us friends as well as her bosses. She will be getting married next summer, and she has already asked me to help with some of the planning since I am a wedding coordinator at our church. It is nice to realize that she values my opinion."

While Susan's office sounds like an appealing place to work, you may find yourself in a very different company culture: professional but politely distant. Some women discover that it is hard to be friends with people they supervise, or they don't want to get too caught up with colleagues because the office culture has an ingrained sense of competition. For other women there's the issue of whom to befriend. In some offices, you may find few other women in supervisory ranks; most of the other women are assistants or secretaries. What does it do for your office image to socialize with them? Many women find that a cordial but not chummy approach works best.

Of course, in some offices, partying together is a nonissue because clearly business is business and fun is fun and never the twain shall meet. Perhaps that was why was Karen Shriver was the only one singing "Happy Birthday" when the cake came out for a colleague in the office. "We had a team meeting this morning and the director brought someone a birthday cake. I sang 'Happy Birthday' and no one joined in. Is that an old lady thing to do?" asks this thirty-four-year-old mother of two from Fairmont, West Virginia. "Are they too cool to sing 'Happy Birthday'?"

See No Evil, Hear No Evil, Speak No Evil

Most of us don't even think about the age issue when we return because we prepared ourselves intellectually. Some have returned to school for degrees in new fields, others have taken brushup courses. Generally you think of expertise, not age, until you see what your coworkers are wearing and saying. You feel like that classic trio of chimpanzees, wanting to put your hands over your eyes, ears, and mouth. "I didn't think about age when I started," says Karen Shriver. "And then I saw what everyone was wearing. That was how I could tell. They all wear hip huggers and bell bottoms. When I was growing up they didn't dress like that." At an office party, Karen skeptically turned to her husband, Dean, and asked, "Do you think anyone is close to my age?"

Susan Seigel's workplace is a high school science classroom, where everything is decidedly different from when she was a student. First there is the subject matter, high school biology, which is at the level she learned in college. Next there is the difference in their dress. "I wouldn't even tell you what they wear sometimes," says Susan, herself a dissident in high school who wore pants as a protest against having to wear skirts. And while she does say that attitude is dramatically different in today's classroom, she has few discipline problems.

After years of threatening to wash Junior's mouth out with soap, moms returning to work might be startled to find that four-letter words sprinkle the conversation in some offices. Casual clothes are nothing compared to the banter. Some businesses, like the financial industry, are known for a macho, back-slapping, letting-it-all-hang-out-to-get-the-client approach. Watch in your initial interviews for cues about office culture. Be aware of what you're heading into.

A twentysomething friend recounted, "One of my husband's coworkers swears all the time, and they've recently had a new hire in their office—a woman in her forties. She complained about all the swearing, and the coworker has had to watch his mouth. My husband and his coworker totally thought she was overreacting, and on her side, I'm sure she was amazed by this behavior."

And curses are not the only colorful language you may encounter. Gen Y has their own words, with "awesome" topping the charts and the ubiquitous "whatever." A miniguide to some other favorites:

Good: phat; killer; dope; we rock, rocked; sweet, as in I'm going on a sweet business trip

Bad: we/it bombed (if said presentation went poorly); sucked; lameass, lame; retarded; loser

The rowdy language is not all that you might have to contend with. Dr. Michele Bolton, a partner in ExecutivEdge, a career-consulting company in Los Gatos, California, has found that in many companies the executive level is still male dominated, with upward of 80 percent men in senior positions. So if you are lucky enough to find yourself sitting around a conference table, you may witness all these men acting like, well, men. What should you do: Adapt and improvise? Leave? "You have to make some compromises to survive in a culture where the expected norms and tradition are male," says Dr. Bolton. Suppose a male colleague tells you the unvarnished truth about your performance, or starts pounding on his desk when something goes wrong. Dr. Bolton urges conciliation to a point. "Your compromise is to be more assertive. Like the men, learn to say 'I' more than 'we.' Become less indirect. Don't say 'I'm sorry' when you mean to say 'Excuse me' to interrupt someone speaking." So adopt some of the male techniques without acting completely like a guy. "You can't give up a part of yourself. It's not a good idea to completely mimic a style that is inauthentic."

Have You Forgotten . . . the Boss from Hell?

One thing you'll find unchanged in the office is the boss from hell. Remember your first or second job, and the guy or gal who made your life miserable. Despite enlightened management training, some misfits still survive. You may have jumped into a job only to discover that the supervisor in question is passive-aggressive, verbally abusive, or just downright evil.

One of Mary's graduate students, Mackenzie Dawson Parks, came back to school after a spell in the cold corporate culture. We asked her to describe the different kinds of difficult managers, who can make your workday a living hell. Here are some types that any human resources executive is familiar with:

- **The Beck-and-Call Boss.** This person is on a power trip, and you're the serf. He or she says, "Jump!" and it's your job to ask, "How high?"
- **The Sleaze.** Sexual harassment laws might be in effect across the country, but the harassment problem still remains. The Sleaze, although some are more overt than others, is the boss who invades your space and makes inappropriate innuendos.
- **The Bipolar Manager.** This is your best friend and your worst enemy all rolled up in one. When she's up, she's up, inviting you to chat in her office and taking you out to lunch. When she's down, she takes you down too, so watch out!
- **The Passive-Aggressive Exec.** Oh, this one's tough. You'll never know what he's really thinking, and while his behavior might say one thing, his words will say something else.
- **The Verbal Abuser.** This manager is just plain mean. Shouting, yelling, sending scathing e-mails, he or she likes to make you feel stupid and usually is quite good at it.

So what do you do when the mere sight of your manager makes you cringe every morning? First, try the same tactics you use with your children. We moms know how to push our kids' buttons, so play amateur shrink and do the same with your boss. That is to say, study your boss and closely observe how she reacts to things. What seems to make her happy? What really pushes her over the top? Is there someone else in your office who gets along really well with her? It might be worth your time to study that person, noticing what she is doing and why it's working.

Try to see his good side. It's easy to turn an evil boss into a demon in your mind, and while picturing Evil Bob with a pitchfork may be amusing, it's not going to improve your attitude. You convey a lot through facial expressions and body language without even realizing it, and smart supervisors are able to sense your dislike, which may make them feel threatened and uncomfortable. Difficult though it may be, try to focus on the good side of your boss. If there's something he is great at, ask questions about it! A little flattery never hurts. Focusing on the positive points will make it easier for you to spend time together, and you won't wear yourself out with negative energy.

If you've tried all this and nothing seems to work, it may be time to have a good old-fashioned chat with your boss. While some people prefer to go straight to human resources, it's probably a better idea to start by dealing with your boss one-on-one. E-mail your boss to set up a meeting, explain what the meeting is for, and include a few points you plan to cover. Don't bullet out a list of accusations; instead put a positive spin on them. For example, "I think we were both disappointed with the way last week's presentation turned out. I feel that maybe we had different expectations, and I'd like to hear your thoughts on it so that we can make sure the next presentation is great."

Still no dice? You may need to bring in an HR director for a three-way discussion. Try not to get emotional, as this will only put your supervisor on the defensive. And think before you speak; it's hard to repair something that is blurted out in anger. Apart from that, sit tight and start checking the want ads.

I Have to Leave by Four P.M. for Junior's Big Soccer Game

The company said it was family-friendly. Now you've hit soccer season and your sixteen-year-old expects you to be at all his games. But there are twenty games on the schedule and you doubt the company is that family-friendly. What do you do? Find a compromise. Work out a deal with Pelé, agreeing to be on the sidelines for his key games.

Terry Nolan of Milford, Connecticut, lucked out. The woman whom she works for loves children, although she has none of her own. Terry says that the fortysomething owner of Advanced Placement has a philosophy that if people are happy with their family life and home life, they give their best to the company. There are nine employees at Advanced Placement, six of whom have children. "All the people are dedicated to work and are also dedicated to their family. If I had not been in this situation, it would have been much harder," says Terry.

Terry loved her former job at the Kennedy Center as a technical support person helping to solve annoying computer problems. She was devoted to her career, but before motherhood her mind-set was very different. "When I was working at my other job full-time, and without a family, my focus was on the work and I worked a lot of hours. I think they had a lot of respect for family there, but I didn't get to test it. If I went back there, it would be hard to break out of the norm. I would have tried to keep up and it would be hard for me."

One of the games that some moms play is hide-and-seek when it comes to flextime. It's two P.M. and the lunch crowd is just wandering back in. You grabbed a yogurt at your desk and are racing to beat the clock so you can finish your work and leave at three. You're on flextime; that's your deal; you negotiated it. You're not doing anything wrong, so why do you feel like you want to quietly crawl out of the office? We have even heard of women leaving their suit jacket on the chair, so it would look like they were still around, not gone for the day.

The guilt. Yes, but you need to get over it. It's important for you and others in the office to accept the reality that you are not leaving early—this is your scheduled departure time. Unfortunately, if most of the office is not on flextime and you are, often others will ignore those boundaries. One mom who was off two days a week told us how she continually got phone calls from the office on her at-home days, sometimes important, sometimes not. One day she got a call in the midst of a toddler's birthday party. She admits she yelled into the phone, "Don't you know I am not working today? I have screaming children in the house." While flexibility requires you to bend a bit, you can set limits. Some mothers communicate with the office via e-mail, which they check once or twice on the off day. If it's an emergency, they respond; otherwise, they wait until the next office day. It seems to work for them.

Almost every mom with a flexible schedule commented that it

was win-win, because they benefited and so did the office. Do not sell yourself short. If you are doing a good job on flextime, there's no need to be on the defensive when someone questions you. One good way to keep on top of the situation is to schedule regular feedback sessions with your boss every six months. If the situation is living up to both your expectations, great, or if not, discuss how it could be improved.

Do They Want Too Much of You? Blurring the Work-Family Boundary

Yes, technology allows you to be in touch with people in different time zones, answer e-mails after the kids are asleep, or prepare a presentation when there is no noise in the house. But technology can be like termites. You don't always see them but you know they're there. That computer looms large behind the closed door in your home office or on the dining room table. You want to shoot off one more e-mail. Your cell phone is on mute, but the LCD says NEW MESSAGE. *Click-click.* A new e-mail arrived, and you are no longer interested in Playdough or puzzles. You say to the kids, "Give me a minute to check my e-mail," and then return two videos later. Technology makes it easier to work from home, but it has also blurred the work-family boundary. "What then happens is that you are not focusing anywhere, and everything gets messed up," says Dr. Dawn Carlson. "Study after study shows that you can't focus and you become horribly guilty because you're trying to balance. Sometimes when I am playing with blocks, I am wondering should I be working, and vice versa."

"Tech flex," as it is called in *Beyond Juggling*, brings to the table many options that make life easier for working moms. But does it really make you a more efficient worker and better mother? Well, maybe not. People who establish boundaries between work and family are actually more connected to their families than those who integrate their jobs and personal life, according to a recent study by Ellen Ernst Kossek, professor of labor and industrial relations at Michigan State University. The study focused on two types of people: those who "integrate" work and family, and those who "separate." Which are you? Do you use the same e-mail for both, the same calendar, the same key chain, the family computer rather than your own?

"Switching back and forth between work and family means you can't give full attention to either, so you're not as effective as you'd like to be," says Professor Kossek. "You're in a no-man's-land." One simple solution, she suggests, is to have a separate space for your work—not the kitchen table—where you can close the door, signaling that you are working—or not. You can also close the door at the end of your day, whatever time that is, signaling to yourself that work is over. One of the problems of working at home, contrary to some employers' beliefs, is not that you will do too little work. Rather, you never stop working, putting some finishing touches on a presentation on Sunday, checking e-mail after the eleven P.M. news. Boundaries help you be a better mother and a better worker.

A lot also depends on the children's ages. Young children need you to focus on them and their needs when they come home from school. With teens, perhaps being in the same house is enough. In fact, knowing teens' uncanny knack for interrupting, many moms of teens use the late afternoons for answering e-mails, tying up loose ends, and other tasks that don't require intense concentration.

Second-Guessing Your Decision

You're back in the office and things are chugging along. The children are all present and accounted for—at least most of the time. You have a flexible work schedule. You even managed to impress your boss with your work on a project. And then it hits you: You could have been the boss, or maybe the boss's boss, if you hadn't back-burnered your career. Growing up we were told that we could be the president one day, or cure cancer, or work hard to afford a nice house and a nice car and nice vacations. But no one ever utters the truth about what happens when children enter that equation and your career derails.

Sitting in her office in tropical Saipan, Vicki King finds satisfaction representing her needy clients. But sometimes she wonders what if she hadn't taken a time-out. "My boss, whom I really like, is very supportive but has always worked full-time. We are about the same age. She is the director; I am the new entry-level staff attorney, digging myself slowly out of debt. I loved staying home, but I definitely traded some important things for that time at home. I'm not sure women who didn't make that choice can really understand that."

One way some women deal with this nagging thought is to consider the flip side of the coin. Suppose you never stopped working. Think of what you would have missed with your children. Think of how you wouldn't have changed as a person because of that experience. Many times in life you are forced to make a decision; don't keep second-guessing yourself about the fork in the road you didn't take. Yes, perhaps by staying home you did take the road less traveled. You are at a different destination now. Deal with that reality, not what could have been.

When it comes to second-guessing, career consultant Michele Bolton advises simply, "Get over it and start exploring what different choices are open to you now. Never have a single idea. You need to have a couple of different ideas. Take negatives and turn them around to positives."

Pat Appleton did just that. Pat joined the U.S. Air Force right out of school and was trained as a Korean linguist. After the birth of the first of her three children, she quit her job and home-schooled her children as her husband, also in the air force, was transferred to various bases around the country. "I liked being in the air force and I liked the work. It was for the children's betterment that I stayed home, not because I didn't like work." After fourteen years at home, she decided to return to the air force as a reservist. She could have gone back as a linguist, but she made a "conscious decision" not to because her rank would be so much lower than that of her former colleagues. "Everyone I had gone to technical school with was now a senior master sergeant and I would have been just an airman. I didn't know if I would be uncomfortable in that situation."

But instead of focusing on the negative, Pat put a positive spin on it. During her time at home, her son, a computer whiz, taught her how to build a Web site and use other software. Pat started back part-time and before long was designing Web sites for the Pentagon for two different air force offices. When her active duty commitment ended and the family moved from Texas to Florida, Pat was hired as a systems developer for a software company, writing programs for public safety and justice departments around the country. She's also working on a systems management degree. Pat admits that the new job is "a real ego boost." Pat didn't look back, lamenting she was left behind. She focused on what she learned while at home and launched an exciting new career that she is sure will challenge and reward her for years to come.

Ambition: It's Back!

You're back at work for six months or so and you look around at your colleagues. That self-doubt you might have harbored about being able to compete again has faded. Or maybe you were confident to begin with and as you settle into the job you realize that you can start to climb upward—again. It's back: ambition!

Some women are surprised. They want a good job and they get it, but now they want more. Carolyn Hoyt needed a job for additional income and health insurance. She was thrilled when she was offered a part-time position as a senior editor at *Working Mother* magazine. Initially her main concern was handling the assignments, not climbing up the masthead. "I was fairly ambitious before I had children, and having children had completely wiped it out. My ambition became to be the best possible mother," she says.

Carolyn quickly became adept at her new position. On her long bus commute, her thoughts often wandered to the possibilities. "I started to think, 'I wouldn't mind running a magazine. I could do that. I am thirty-six now. I wonder how long it would take to become an editor?' Sitting on the bus, I mentally pulled back and thought, 'What's that all about?' The whole idea of working was to get health insurance, not to become editor in chief."

Carolyn was emboldened by her easy transition back to the office. After two years, the magazine owners let go the entire staff and brought in a new editorial board, so Carolyn never had a chance to play out her fantasy. Now once again a successful freelance writer, she is satisfied with the notion that when and if the time comes for a full-time position, she can succeed and then some.

Carolyn's experience was typical of many moms we interviewed. These women found that that motto we often tell our children, "Success begets success," is also true for them. That was Debbie Mahoney's experience when she returned to work in a part-time clerical position at Mercy Medical Center in Rockville Centre, New York. It wasn't long before she was looking for more challenges. "Once I regained my confidence and saw that I was capable of learning anything and everything they threw at me, I knew I wanted to achieve more. It became apparent to me that with some extra effort I would be able to excel. I wanted to excel in something other than being someone's wife and mother, which is common, I'm sure, for a lot of women. It was very satisfying to have professionals rely on me and compliment me on a job well done."

This is particularly impressive considering that Debbie thought about quitting after the first month because she was so intimidated by the many changes that had occurred in the office during her fifteen years at home. After working a number of years, she gradually added more responsibilities and more days and passed the arduous exam to become a certified medical staff coordinator. Debbie now holds dual positions. She's an administrative assistant to the hospital's medical executive committee as well as program coordinator for a women's health initiative, which involves marketing the hospital's services to local area doctors.

The second time around, ambition seems to be fueled by an inner drive rather than competing against others. We prove that we can succeed, indeed shine, and it's almost as if we are challenging and competing with ourselves. "The more I felt personally satisfied, the more I wanted!" says Debbie. Somehow we don't think this is the end of her success story, or Carolyn's, or some of the scores of other women we have met.

DOS AND DON'TS OF THE WORKPLACE IN THE TWENTY-FIRST CENTURY

- Do make friends with a fifteen-year-old computer geek who can be your tech teacher . . . shortly after you leave the delivery room.
- Do fool around on the Internet and learn to find information and new Web sites and links.
- Don't say, "Show me the Smith Corona." Your boss may think you are an alcoholic.
- Don't look at the computer and say, "I hardly know how to work a VCR."
- Don't be Ms. Schoolmarm and come across as a curmudgeon just because you meet deadlines early.
- Don't look prissy. Go up the down staircase once in a while.
- Don't play Mom and volunteer to bake the cookies for the holidays, or give advice to the lovelorn.

Seven

Getting the Job

IT TOOK MONTHS OR MAYBE YEARS and, finally, you are ready to go back. Your head is swimming. There will be endless arrangements to make, from rescheduling car pools to writing lists of instructions to getting backups for the backups. But first, there are two big hurdles to clear: Writing your résumé and getting through the job interview.

You have been out of work for a few years or more, and get a case of the shakes when you think about composing a résumé. "How can I write, 'Work experience: 1990–present: zip'?" Sure, it's frustrating, but before you start ripping up the résumé and tossing it in the trash, consider ways to get around the black hole. Focus on what exactly a résumé is supposed to do. A résumé will not get you a job. The whole purpose of a résumé is to provide a snapshot of you (a flattering one, please!) so that you get called for an interview. Think of a résumé as "employable you at a glance," because a glance is all it will get in the first go-around. Classified advertisements, especially on Internet job boards, can generate hundreds of résumés in response, and the initial look is probably a minute or less . . . unless your résumé is deliberately plucked from the pile. The single best way to make that happen is to network. Networking is so important that we rank it before the résumé and interview, because odds are you won't make the first cut without some personal contacts.

Networking

How do you network? As we made clear early on, it is important to keep in touch with people in your former industry or make contacts in your new field. A few ideas beyond e-mails and phone calls: attend conferences and lectures; take a class and don't be shy, introduce yourself to speakers, and follow up. Nothing beats the personal touch, and most people are flattered by, "I enjoyed your talk." Call friends of friends; ask if anyone knows anyone in the career that interests you. Then call them. Yes, it takes some nerve, but it does get easier over time.

Once you make a contact, ask for recommendations of other people to talk to and then use the first person as a reference to the second. Identify places where you would like to work and then try to get an appointment for an informational interview. Talk is cheap and everyone likes to give advice. That's the key: You don't want to be blatant and say, "Hire me." Instead you are looking for advice on how to achieve that ambition. Mary had a friend who wanted to work at a major New York newspaper but didn't have the credentials to start there. Nonetheless, the friend made contact with a high-level editor and told him about her goals. They started an e-mail correspondence. It took five years, but the woman worked her way up through a midsized newspaper and then a larger newspaper, sending articles she had written to the editor every six months or so. When the New York newspaper expanded, she was hired. You can use the same techniques while you are in school or working part-time. Set a goal for yourself and figure out who can help you reach that goal.

Part of an overall job strategy is to look for your first *and* second job at the same time. Think about how that "starter" job will prepare you to go for the plum position a few years down the road. Whom do you need to meet to get your name out there? Also don't be shy about letting nonbusiness acquaintances know your goals. Make that backyard barbeque at your neighbor's work for you. You never know whom you will meet standing around the grill. By the time you are ready to actively look for a job, your agenda should have several dozen names and numbers of people you can contact.

The Résumé

Mary once applied for a writing position listed in the classifieds with a résumé that was printed on ivory paper. She thought she had the perfect qualifications but never heard back. Through her network of business acquaintances she found someone who knew the hiring editor and called him on her behalf. It turned out the editor liked only résumés on white paper and had tossed Mary's. She sent a new résumé (on white paper) and got the job. You may shake your head in disbelief and question who would want to work for that boss, anyway, but we have heard several such tales about strange methods for sorting through piles of résumés.

There's lots of advice on résumés out there, and sometimes it is contradictory. Some experts believe, for example, you should include an "objective" at the top of your résumé such as, "I seek a challenging sales position that will allow me to maximize my potential and income." We see two problems with that: first, who wouldn't like a job that will maximize personal and economic growth? Second, you have just eliminated yourself from every nonsales job.

As adjunct manager for the NYU journalism department, Mary hires about twenty new part-time professors each semester to add to her roster of about thirty "regulars." She sees dozens of résumés every year and interviews upward of fifty people annually. Often she receives a résumé with the objective as a "full-time position." Yet Mary hires only for part-time slots and she replies with a letter stating such. Often the full-time job seeker responds with a phone call saying that she will consider part-time. In the meantime someone else has been hired. So don't take yourself out of the running before you even begin. Leave off the objective. If you feel that you must write an objective, work it into a cover letter.

There is also disagreement among some experts on whether to write a chronological or a functional résumé. A chronological résumé lists jobs by dates in reverse time order. A functional résumé lists skills grouped in categories such as supervisory, leadership, interpersonal, research, communication, sales, customer service, problem solving, team building and so on. Some experts like Wendy Enelow, coauthor of *Expert Résumés for People Returning to Work,*[1] recommend the functional résumé for moms with large gaps in employment.

She suggests formatting the résumé with two columns of bulleted items, highlighting your skills and qualifications. "By isolating these at the beginning, someone gets a good snapshot of who you are," says Wendy, founder of Career Masters Institute in Lynchburg, Virginia. "The returnee's résumé must be skills focused. It must bring to the forefront any skills and qualifications from previous work experience (no matter how long ago it was), from community and school-based activities, and from managing a household."

This is the last time we will say it: Get out that agenda . . . again. List every volunteer and community service position from the past years. If you have trouble recollecting, think chronologically, using your children's grades as a guide: preschool, first grade, and so on. Now become your own spin doctor. If this is difficult for you, think about politicians. Don't they tell the story that they want the people to hear? It is no different with your résumé. You're in the driver's seat; steer the résumé in the direction you want it to go. For example, don't say that you coordinated the annual fund-raising for the parents' association at your son's school. Rather, extrapolate and talk about the specific skills—organizational, negotiating, and planning—you needed to do the job. You are, in fact, an experienced events manager. If you raised $5,000, say that. If that $5,000 was a 10 percent increase over the previous year, note that too. Sounds better already, doesn't it?

Wendy says you should decide how you want to be perceived before writing the résumé. Imagine that before children you had a finance degree and worked in sales for a financial products firm. If you are now applying for a job selling travel packages, pump up the sales experience and downplay the degree in finance. "Things like international travel and foreign languages are big selling points and are important in this global economy," says Wendy. "Paint the picture you want someone to see while remaining in the realm of reality." And finally, Wendy says, do not apologize for an absence!

Laura West, president of the Orion Career Group, in Missoula, Montana, sometimes suggests that a client use a chronological résumé with a twist: List previous jobs by length of time: five years, rather than 1990–1995. She too urges moms to list all their nonpaid work. "Do not underestimate the unpaid experience. When I work with mothers returning to work, sometimes they think they have done nothing in their years out that is attractive to employers. That's not true. Volunteer, community, and household work can be very valuable." Laura recalled one client who had been out for fifteen years and wanted to get back into marketing. The client had years of experience fund-raising and event coordinating for her children's school and as a database manager for a soccer club. "On her résumé we were able to translate that volunteer work back to marketing and sales, and she got a job based on that experience."

Functional or chronological, all the experts agree on certain résumé basics:

- Use action verbs like "negotiated," "staffed," "supervised," and "created." They all sound stronger than "worked on."
- Turn experience into percentages or numbers. Instead of saying that you chaired a fund-raiser for the community center,

write that you increased the revenues of the capital campaign by 20 percent.

- Your résumé is the first snapshot the employer has of you, so make the document visually appealing with an attractive layout. Proofread it several times to eliminate spelling errors or typos. It never hurts to have someone else proof it for you as well.

- If you are e-mailing it—and you must if that's what the employer is requesting—print it out first to see how the résumé looks. Don't rely solely on the computer screen version. Also, slug it "Smith résumé" not just résumé. You'll get lost in the attachment file with every other "résumé." Ask for a reply telling you that your e-mailed résumé arrived. It is not unrealistic to fear that your résumé is lost in cyberspace.

- Keep the résumé to one page. Remember, the résumé will get a quick glance and you want your most marketable skills to jump out.

- Find out if the employer uses résumé "scanning." If your résumé is going to be scanned, center your name, address, phone, and e-mail on the top; don't use lines or borders; leave wide margins on all sides; and use white paper. Make sure the words relevant to the position (for example "sales" or "customer service") are in the résumé so they will be picked up in the scan.

A few other tips: Include some select interests and hobbies. We're not sure scrapbooking will impress anyone, but running road races, reading modern British literature, acting in community theater, or playing the piano for church services all help create an image of an active, intellectually engaged woman. So do skills that might not seem job related, like gourmet cooking. A gourmet cook must be able to follow directions carefully, be detail oriented, and have a creative spark, all attributes that are sought after in any number of jobs. Don't forget to include computer skills, especially if you have mastered some software programs.

The résumé should not include every job you ever held. Maybe being a Brownie leader was fun, but making crafts every Friday afternoon doesn't translate into a job skill. Maybe you did temp work for an accountant during tax season, but it was only for a month or so. Think twice about including those short-term jobs. That's what Amy Haller, now coordinator of registration at McHenry County College in Crystal Lake, Illinois, did when she interviewed for full-time work. "I left out the short-term, part-time jobs on my résumé. I didn't want to be pegged as a job hopper and thought that the gaps due to motherhood would be more acceptable."

What's Next?

The résumé is done; maybe you tackled it or you had the help of a professional résumé writer. It's ready to go, but where? One supposedly easy strategy is to apply for every possible job and blanket the market with your résumé. You may get lucky and get a call, but chances are it will be about as easy as winning the lottery. The best way to get a job is to get out that network list and start calling. Sure, it's a lot harder to face outright rejection on the phone than from some faceless company in cyberspace. However, don't ignore the Internet job boards, because they can give you an overview of openings in your field and the particular skills in demand. You can then tailor your search with that information in mind.

You must make contact with a person, either in the human resources department or in the department where you want to work. In either case, even if you are told there are no openings, ask if you can send your résumé along and then come in for an "informational interview." Bernadette Cain of Bay Shore, New York, looking for a job in hospital administration, went for an informational interview in New York City. There were no openings, but the administrator liked her background and suggested that Bernadette call the program director in another hospital on Long Island where she'd heard there might be an opening. Bernadette used the first administrator's name to open the door at the second hospital, where she eventually got a great job. The lesson? Always ask your contact if there's anyone he or she can recommend, and keep thinking six degrees of separation. It really does work.

Once you have the name of a contact, send out your résumé and a cover letter. (Please make sure it is spelled correctly; never assume a spelling even on a conventional name. And don't assume the gender. Jordan, Blair, Morgan: Ms. or Mr.?) Forget about a one-size-fits-all cover letter. The one-page letter must be tailored to each situation. If there's a specific opening, tell why you are the right person to fill that opening. If there are no openings, explain why you want to work at that particular company. Reinforce your strengths by reiterating an item from the résumé. Mary often receives over-the-transom résumés from professional journalists who point out in the cover letter some teaching background that is not immediately apparent from the professional résumé, or they expand on some foreign assignments or particular reporting that makes them well suited to teach a specific class.

So whether it's through a classified, a contact, or someone you met at the supermarket checkout line, you finally have an interview. The next step is to thoroughly research the company before you go to the interview. You've asked your own kids endless times, "Did you do your homework?" Now it's your turn. We can guarantee that during the interview something will be referenced that you will not know if you didn't do your homework. Start by browsing the potential employer's Web site. What information does it feature? What company news or achievements are highlighted? Go beyond the first page and read deep into the site. Try to find out the company's goals so you can tailor your interview to helping them expand their market share or improve their communications or start a new project. "Research ahead of time is crucial for knowing how to answer questions, what kind of bottom line results are sought, what kinds of problems need solving, and what benefit and value you can bring to the company," says Laura West. "For a woman trying to get back into marketing, for example, let's say the company is trying to expand market share. She can bring up marketing-related past volunteer work with specific examples and numbers where possible." Ask your local librarian for help in running a check of newspaper and magazine articles on the company. You should always go armed with information about the company, its culture, its organization, its accomplishments and goals. It can make an indelible impression on an interviewer if during the course of conversation your comments indicate that you have done your homework.

The reverse is also true. Mary will never forget asking a job seeker what course he would like to teach. He answered, "I don't know. I didn't look at the course catalog yet." Mary was too polite to end the interview then and there, but that's what she wanted to do. It may seem like a lot of work to prepare for an interview, but remember that cliché: You have one chance to make a good first impression.

The Interview

The interview is your next challenge. Interviews are nothing new to any of us. The first question most of us ask, as we rip apart the closet, is what to wear? If you haven't worked in a while, you may be clueless, especially when you see your neighbor run out to work every day in a sweater, khaki pants, and flip-flops. Forget it. For an interview, the old rules still apply. Business attire works for an interview even if the company culture is twenty-first-century casual. You may be surprised to learn that some large accounting firms still have shoe codes prohibiting open toes and mules. Please leave at home those gorgeous jangling earrings that you got for Mother's Day. And speaking of noise, since you may be a bit nervous, check that your cell phone is off . . . twice. The last thing you need is a call from Junior telling you that he forgot his lunch.

When it comes to dressing for an interview, erring on the side of conservatism can't hurt, but you don't want to look like you just came from a time warp. If you are applying for a job in a creative industry, it's okay to dress a bit trendier without being outrageous. Leave yourself plenty of time to get to the interview location early, but don't show up in the actual office more than ten minutes in advance.

Before you go to interview for your dream job, see if you can set up some trial runs. By this we mean arrange to go on an interview for a job that doesn't really interest you. You will feel more at ease when the real deal comes along, plus you'll become more comfortable with your answers to the stock questions. Those queries are the basis for most interviews, so if you prepare in advance you'll be relaxed enough to tailor them to your particular situation. When the interviewer opens with, "Tell me a little about yourself," don't start by saying, "I was born in 19 . . ." Some returnees may avoid that pitfall because they don't want to tell their age, and instead their answer starts with, "I am the mother of four boys." Forget it. As much as you want to share family photos with the person on the other side of the desk, it's a poor strategy. The only snapshot you should show is in the form of your two-minute verbal biography, highlighting your own skills and why you are a good match for the particular job.

Another stock question is a variation on "Why do you want to work here?" or "Why do you think you're qualified for this job?" The interviewer is really asking, "Why should I hire you?" It helps to focus on three main points about your background, skills, and goals to answer those questions. You want to work at a particular company because you admire the product or service, you have background and/or education in that field, and you will utilize certain skills in that particular position. Don't use the word "win-win" but try to work that concept into your answer. Why will it be both a win for you and the company if you are hired for a particular position? The trick is to turn generalizations into specifics. Make file cards with the key points, but do not try to memorize them and do not bring them with you! Except for some off-the-wall question designed to test your ability to think on your feet, you should have the answer ready to almost every question. You need to be relaxed and comfortable with your answers, not sounding like you are reading a cue card.

One of our least favorite stock questions is, "Tell me your worst trait . . . or your biggest weakness . . . or your biggest failure." Resist the temptation to reply with some snappy rejoinder. Instead, come back with a positive "weakness," like working too hard or being too detail oriented. Then tell how you handle those weaknesses: You learned to stop working after eight hours and come back fresh the next day. Or you step back from a project for a day or so and then view it with a clear eye.

While it is illegal to ask questions about your private life that do not impact on the job, that doesn't stop some interviewers from fishing around. You could say, "That question is illegal and I don't have to answer it." Instead, if you want the job, try to find out what the interviewer really wants to know. A question about child care may be a way of finding out whether you can travel or work long hours. Answer truthfully. If you can and are willing to travel, simply say that your child-care arrangements can accommodate travel. If you don't want to travel, then say so.

Some questions could turn out to be stumbling blocks if you are not prepared for them. Here is our list of the top ten most feared questions and how to answer them.

1. **Don't you think you are overqualified?**

   This is the time to answer a question with a question. Career counselor Monique LaCour of Career Management Services suggests responding, "Overqualified? Tell me what the fear is?" Wait briefly for the answer (usually there is an inadequate explanation) and then continue: "Quite frankly, I can do that job and then some. If the fear is that I am going to get bored, actually, I am dedicated and I don't start a project that I don't complete. I am the person you can spread a little more thinly. You get more than your money's worth." When the interviewer suggests that you are underqualified, perhaps because of your time out, ask him or her to explain what "qualified" is, suggests Monique. "Lots of times the interviewer can't really explain it and you can counter that actually you have been able to excel in those areas in less than their required time, and reference examples."

2. **How do you explain the ten-year gap in employment?**

   This is a no-brainer. Simply say, "I took time off to raise my children." In this case, less is more. If you feel compelled, you can add that you are excited to resume your career, that all arrangements are in place, and that you are looking forward to getting started . . . at this company.

3. **What will you do if your child-care person is a no-show?**

   Your child-care arrangements should be in order prior to the interview. And don't have just one plan. Always have a backup plan in place, but don't go into detail. Besides making the interviewer feel more secure about offering you the job, it shows that you are the kind of woman who thinks ahead, a good planner. Of course, we knew that about ourselves years ago.

4. **Do you mind reporting to a boss ten years younger than you?**

For years you have been handling your kids' temper tantrums, stubbornness, and occasionally downright unreasonable behavior. Dealing with a boss whom you consider childish will be a cinch. As for the answer, simply, "No. I respect competence and seniority and have no problem dealing with a boss who is ten years younger."

The tougher challenge will be dealing with a boss your own age, who also has three children but never left the workplace to be an at-home mom. She may not have had the option or may have chosen not to take time off from her career. It's possible she will be resentful or even jealous.

5. **Is your husband glad you're going back to work? I bet he is!**

This question is loaded with financial nuances. Perhaps the guy in the other chair wishes his wife would go back and bring home a second income. Begin by saying that your husband has always been supportive of your choices and that yes, he is glad, because this was a decision that you made together. The worst thing you can convey is that there is any sort of dissension between you and your husband regarding this decision. It will put up a red flag and the interviewer will immediately wonder how you are going to make this work without support from your family, beginning with your spouse.

6. **What do you think about the president's foreign policy?**

Assuming that you are not being interviewed at the White House, it is legitimate to ask, "What does this has to do with the job?" But a better response is "For everyone's sake, I hope he can bring about world peace." Don't continue this conversation, and control yourself from initiating any other politically loaded or controversial discussion. The interviewer doesn't need to know your views on abortion and gun control.

7. **Are you expecting to have more children?**

There are questions that are illegal to ask, yet it is very possible that the interviewer will weave them into the conversation in a chummy, casual manner. An illegal question gives legitimacy to an elusive answer like, "We are very pleased with our three sons."

8. **Will this part-time job be intellectually challenging enough?**

Assure the interviewer that you have carefully thought out your career plans and this part-time job will certainly keep you challenged as you reenter the workforce. It is wise to assure the interviewer that if you thought you were going to be bored, you wouldn't apply for the job. This is the right position for this point in your life and the foreseeable future.

9. **If you could be an animal or a fruit or a car, what would you choose?**

While this may sound like those stupid questions asked of Miss America finalists, be prepared to give an answer that puts you in a good light. Our advice is to stay away from the fruits and the animals and go for the car, perhaps an SUV that has a good record for safety, reliability, and versatility, or a sleek sports car that possesses lots of zip and drive. Keep it short and simple, and smile. The supposed point of these questions is to see how you think out of the box. A newspaper article noted that one job candidate was asked to give the sum of all numbers from 1 to 99, and the poor guy was actually going to try to add them! How about instead, "Do you have a calculator?"

10. **Where do you want to be in five years?**

A generalized answer is good for this. "I'd like to be in a challenging position with this company, with more responsibility."

Bottom line: Keep in mind that your goal in the interview is to present yourself as a serious, smart woman who is willing to work hard to get her career restarted. You're energetic, easy to work with, and can be both a leader and a team member, depending on what the situation calls for. It's that simple.

When the interviewer is finished tossing questions to you, it is your turn. Ask the interviewer to describe an average day, to tell about the specific skills required. Listen carefully and try to point out later in the conversation that you possess some of these same skills. Ask about the last person who held this job. Where did he or she go? It can help you ascertain a career track from that position—or lack of one. You might ask about other staffers or clients whom you will interact with daily or weekly. This is *not* the time to ask about salary or vacation or benefits. Save that for the second interview. Before you leave, inquire about the next step in the process and when you can expect to hear back. And, finally, remember what Mom taught you: Write a thank-you note.

BUT MAYBE MOM WAS WRONG ABOUT A FEW OTHER POINTS

While "listen to Momma" is good advice, Drs. Ron and Caryl Krannich, the authors of 35 career books,[2] suggest that maybe she was wrong about a few points:

- *Do* talk to strangers. Networking is the number-one way to find a job, and that means approaching strangers. "You must go beyond your buddies," Ron says.
- *Do* discuss money. If you want to find out what a job pays, you need to ask questions. If you can't find out and an interviewer asks about your "salary needs," turn the question around and ask, "What would someone with my qualifications usually earn?"
- *Do* talk about yourself. "Toot your own horn," says Ron. The purpose of an interview is to focus on your worth to the employers, rather than what they can give you. Once you demonstrate your value, you can then focus on getting paid what you are worth.

Negotiating Time and Money

You made the first cut and you're asked back for a second interview. Chances are the company will now be trying to convince *you* that it's a great place to work. This is your opportunity to do some negotiating.

If you want flexible scheduling, don't be afraid to ask for it. Too many women take themselves out of the game without even trying to play. One friend of ours, who has been mulling a return to work, lamented, "I'll never find a decent-paying job with flexible hours." Don't be a mind reader. You have no idea what a potential boss will say. In a survey, Flexible Resources, Inc., found with their clients that only 38 percent of baby boomers asked their former employers for a flexible schedule, as opposed to 53 percent of Gen Xers. Perhaps we all can learn something from our younger sisters!

The timing of asking for flex needs to be calibrated carefully. Kirsten Ross, head of Womans-Work.com, an organization that helps women find alternative work arrangements, believes that you don't ask about flexible scheduling until you have "wowed" them. "Don't bring it up until they are trying to sell the organization to you," says Kirsten. "Then ask, 'Are you willing to consider alternative work arrangements at all?' The timing of this is tricky. It must be right in between selling yourself and them offering you the job." Pat Katepoo, founder of WorkOptions.com in Kaneohe, Hawaii, agrees. "When they start selling you and the benefits they offer, and if they mention telecommuting or flexible work arrangements, probe more about it and ask about the levels of usage." Often this takes place at the second or third round of interviews.

If you must have flextime to balance work with your family, don't settle for simply getting the job; try to get the job on your own terms. Don't make excuses about why you need flextime. Just ask for it. If the answer you get is a quick no, then take a second look at the company. What are they going to say when Junior has 104-degree fever and you need time off to take him to the doctor? Take a tip from labor lawyer Kathryn Poling, who negotiated a thirty-hour workweek with the Defense Department. "If you make an unusual demand and they say, 'Sorry we can't bend,' do you really want to be working for them?"

We know several women who signed on for a job with hopes that once they "proved" themselves there would be more flexibility. It never happened! Kathryn advises women to do their homework before making a request. If you know an organization has flextime, decide in advance exactly what your terms are. Be prepared, for example, if you ask for three-quarters time, to agree to three-quarters salary. Or if you want flextime, draw up a schedule of how you will put in the required hours. You might propose on-site work Tuesday, Wednesday, and Thursday from seven A.M. to three P.M. and telecommuting the other two days. Another somewhat unusual idea, suggested by Monique, is to ask the company to consider contracting to you a major portion of the job so you can do it on a flex schedule. The remainder of the work could be farmed out within the company. The key is to have your answers ready and be armed with a well-prepared proposal for the flexible schedule.

Kathryn needed to work a much-reduced schedule for the first two months because her husband was still stationed in Colorado when she made the move to Washington, D.C. She needed time to set up the new house, find schools for the children, and attend to the myriad other details a move involves. Again, the Defense Department agreed—if she could work out a plan. She came prepared: She told them she would take "unpaid leave" on the days she was not at work for the first two months, and then go to a thirty-hour flextime workweek. You can do the same. Run it up the flagpole and see if anyone salutes. You may be surprised.

One caveat: While the human resources department may be very happy to offer you a flextime schedule, your immediate boss may not, so make sure you check with him or her. "No matter the culture, the key link to flexibility is the direct boss, and that person will make it work or break it," says Pat Katepoo. Also make sure you're both speaking the same language; at some companies flextime means flexible start/stop hours, at other companies it means telecommuting or compacted workweeks. Pat's Web site, Workoptions.com, offers one-stop shopping for proposing and negotiating flexible work arrangements. She offers a few tips.

- Do some intelligence and look at the industry and its policies. Some businesses, such as communications, banking, and accounting, have policies on the books. If you're applying to a corporation that does not have an official flex policy, try to find other similar companies that do, and use those models.
- Before applying for a job, call HR and get their formal or informal flexibility policy and discern policy vs. practice. Some things look great on paper, but how they are implemented can be very different.
- Remember that flex in its purest form is really a business strategy, not a privilege or a perk. Also keep in mind that it usually doesn't go over well to be a new employee asking for a flexible work arrangement where it hasn't been done before. Wait until you've established yourself for at least six months.
- Beware of signing on for part-time hours where the amount of work is not adjusted to a part-time level.

This second interview is a good time to check out the company culture. Keep your eyes open as you walk around the office: Do people look happy? How they are dressed? Are there family photos around? Are employees conversing with one another? Check out the Web site and annual report one more time and see what the company's public image conveys.

Often the most difficult and stressful part of the job search process is the salary negotiation. That's because women are often afraid to meet the salary discussion head-on. One supervisor at a major company told us, "Women rarely negotiate for a higher salary, while men always do." Mary has found that to be true with adjuncts. Many men, after initially accepting the offer, come back and ask firmly but politely, "Is that the highest you can go?" Women, if they ask at all, seemed inclined to make excuses such as, "I am living on a tight budget and could really use more money," as one told Mary. So many women seem grateful just to get the job.

When it comes to the salary, again, research is important. Try to find out any way you can—through friends, job boards, Internet sites, and magazine listings—what comparable positions pay. Also have a number in mind that is the minimum you will accept. After all, it makes no sense to accept a job that won't cover your expenses and then some, unless it provides you entry into a new field (and then it should be only a short-term situation.) Some moms told us they were asked for a salary history, and when they listed their ten-year-old salary or their part-time salary, the numbers were embarrassingly low. You could simply fill in "not applicable" and see if it flies. Another salary question arises: Should you be paid a beginner's salary or one commensurate with a current employee at the same level? Connie Fuller, a human resources expert and author, says to keep in mind, "Anyone who steps out of the workforce, man or woman, for any reason, will have to deal with the reality that they have had a break in service; this is not a gender issue. It is incumbent upon the candidate to be able to demonstrate that the break in service has not caused her to get behind in the knowledge, awareness, and skills related to the job for which she is applying."

At this point in the interview process you should have convinced the employer that despite your years out you acquired new skills. That should be your bargaining point in asking for a salary appropriate with the job you are asked to perform. If a company feels you can handle the job, then you deserve the salary that goes with that particular job. Monique says, "Your argument should be, 'If you are paying other executives a certain salary and I can come in and do what they do, then I deserve a similar salary.' If they want to offer you a lesser salary, then they better have a good reason. Quite frankly, if someone is offered a beginner's salary for a higher-level job, then she may not be selling herself properly."

Keep in mind also that every job has a range: beginning, middle, and maximum. Perhaps you will come in at the low end of the range as opposed to someone with continuous experience who could command the high end. Be prepared to negotiate on other points, depending on what you need. Perhaps health insurance is not important; you are covered by your husband's plan. Conversely, perhaps your husband is worried about getting downsized, so you may take a lower salary in a job with broad family health coverage.

NEGOTIATING TIME AND MONEY

Sheila Heen of the Harvard Negotiation Project and coauthor of *Difficult Conversations: How to Discuss What Matters Most*[3] offers the following suggestions:

- Don't apologize for your time at home. It's a job: You coordinate projects, coach people, and manage resources. At a paid position you're doing the same tasks, just with colleagues more cooperative than your children!

- Decide your priorities before going to an interview. If money tops the list, consider why. Is it that you need the income? The respect from your colleagues? The status that a certain salary confers? Deciding *why* you put money at the top of the list will help you negotiate to meet your real interests. For example, if they're strapped and status is an issue, a better title, a place on the organizational chart, or an assistant may compensate.

- Go armed with a sword and shield into a salary negotiation. Find the job's salary range through online surveys, networking, or other sources. With that information you can tell the employer, "Here's what it looks like my skills are worth" (the sword), and if they balk you can protect yourself with, "Look, I just want something that's fair" (the shield).

- If time is the number-one priority and the company has never flexed before, don't start with hard-nosed haggling. Begin the discussion as a question: "If I want to work from home one or two days, how could we arrange that?" Make it clear that you care about the employer's needs as well as your own. You want to negotiate a win-win situation.

- If the employer refuses to flex, request that the issue be revisited at a specific future time—say, six months. Be sure to find out why there's no flexibility. If it's a structural reason—you need to be on-site for clients, meetings, etc.—the odds are unfavorable. If it's a matter of trust or policy, once you prove that you are a kick-ass worker, then you can renegotiate.

Closing the Deal

In this age of heightened security, it is not unusual for an employer to conduct a background check, to call all your references, or even to require drug testing. Give your references a heads-up and fill them in on possible questions from the potential employer. A rave recommendation can often clinch the deal. Mary hired a young journalist who had never taught before after one of his graduate school professors enthused about his communication skills and knowledge of the field. The unqualified recommendation erased any doubts. Make sure you have references who will give specific, positive responses. It doesn't help you if a reference says, "Well, I can't really tell you how she would be in a supervisory role because I have never observed her."

How to Keep Making a Good Impression

You got the job! Congratulations. Now what? The first six months and the last six months on a job should be your best. In other words, wow them as you go in and as you leave. Those early months can be a period of major adjustment both on the job and at home. In fact, Loretta likes to say, "Wouldn't it be wonderful if every job could start at month six?" Those first months can be uneasy, but they set the tone for your employment; if you are on flextime, you must make an especially good impression.

If you do get flextime, prove to be a good employee by keeping visible and not isolating yourself. It's a good idea not to advertise that you are on a flex schedule. If someone asks you to make a meeting on a Friday and that's your day off, there's no harm in saying, "Monday is better for me. Can we do it then?" However, be flexible about important meetings. Try to answer your e-mail and voice messages promptly. Pat Katepoo suggests that you "make an aggressive effort in the first six months to see how your flex is impacting everyone, and then make adjustments if necessary and let your boss know about them." Meet all customers and coworkers in the first few months and make sure your work schedule fits their needs.

Don't be misled by the casual office. While the office may be informal, the company still has performance requirements that you need to meet. Monique says, "Don't get too comfortable. You can come in a ponytail but still need to fulfill their expectations." One sure way to do that, she suggests, is to convince the employer that you are going to "add value" and that you are going to make them look good. "The better you make the boss look, the longer you stay in your job." Maybe even get a raise!

Another tip: Try to act calm and collected even if you're anything but, with the adjustment going on at home. Many women going back to work told us they were reeling from all the changes in the first few months. You will get through the shakedown period at home. In the meantime, it helps your work image to look organized, especially if you're not. Even if you write responses to your e-mail on Sunday evening, wait until first thing Monday to send them out. It looks like you are well organized rather than fitting in the work whenever and wherever you can find a free moment.

Finally, be confident. You were hired because someone in a position of authority thought you could do a good job. You've earned this position. Enjoy it, excel, and go forward from here.

Eight

Looking Ahead

AS WE FINISHED THIS BOOK, we sat outside one beautiful summer day reflecting on what we had discovered by interviewing more than one hundred mothers, combing through almost one thousand surveys, and discussing weighty issues such as "gender equality" and women's economic status with some of the country's top experts. What have we learned? The essence is simple: Despite the naysayers, women can move in and out of careers and find economic and emotional rewards. Of course, a strategic game plan puts the odds in your favor. That's what this book details: how to practice, practice, practice while you are out of the game, so you can win when you go back to the playing field.

The other major discovery we made is that the rules of the game are changing in this millennium. As Dr. Myra Hart, a Harvard Business School professor, notes, "I think we are experiencing something entirely new, as this is the first generation of women who feels it is possible to move in and out of the workforce without significant penalties for time out. We don't know how these expectations will play out, but I am optimistically awaiting the next chapter."

That next chapter, so to speak, is being written by you, the pioneers, the mothers who are rejecting the organization-man model and making it up as you go. As we noted in the introduction, your progress will be made easier by several trends: Gen Xers settling for nothing less than flexibility, baby boomers who want to scale back their hours but not retire, and the predicted labor shortage. Dr. Hart is a pioneer herself, getting her MBA in her thirties and becoming one of the founding partners of Staples and then earning her doctorate in her fifties and joining the Harvard Business School faculty. She predicts that yet another trend will make it easier for moms to return to the workforce. "The changes will come not from a tight labor market but from business leaders who recognize that there is real talent pool among these smart women not currently in the workforce, that there is extraordinary talent outside the current workforce." She adds that women business owners, in particular, will recognize this talent pool and find ways to lure women back to challenging jobs that can be performed outside the organization-man mold.

We wholeheartedly agree. When we started researching this book, we easily found woman after woman who had reinvented herself. There are thousands of bright, energetic women who are willing to give their time and talent to the right job. What they ask in return is flexibility in terms of when and how they perform their jobs. "We know that giving workers flexibility and control over how their work is done elicits the most commitment and loyalty. Research also tells us that given flexibility, people are not only more effective, they can work more hours without experiencing work-life conflict," says Susan Seitel, president of Work & Family Connection in Minnetonka, Minnesota.

The visionary business leaders will reap the benefits not only when these women are still hands-on moms, but even more so when the children have flown the coop and the mothers turn their energies to their next project. Changes are already happening just below the radar in woman-owned businesses. We don't know whether the planets were perfectly aligned or it was simply luck, but just as we were finishing this book and predicting the need for workplace changes, we kept encountering pioneers such as a housepainter mom—with a long waiting list of clients—who works during her children's school hours, and an architect who has worked flex hours for years, first to care for her daughter and now so she can have time for herself. One woman, Sally Sarsfield, working part-time as a CFO for her husband's start-up company, was looking to hire other like-minded moms. "We think there is a great untapped resource out there of women with school-aged children who want to work part-time but need more flexibility. We are able to offer that flexibility and hope to be able to attract some high-caliber, part-time employees."

In search of a part-time employee with a financial services background, Sally put up fliers in nursery schools and the local Ys in her hometown of Westport, Connecticut. Ultimately she found a qualified mom through "three degrees of separation" by sending e-mails to everyone she knows. Sally thinks many moms don't look for work because they believe there's nothing available with the flexibility they need. "They are thinking and wishing and wondering, 'What am I going to do when my youngest starts kindergarten?'"

In writing this book we also found that while we spend a lot of time tracking the developmental changes of our children's lives, we pay little attention to the different stages of our own lives, perhaps because this is a newer area of psychology. There's an increasing acknowledgment that adults go through different periods of development too. However, it seems that we plan our careers based on the assumption that our interests and skills will never change. We have found just the opposite; there are many ways to work. The way a new mom works is different from the way a mom of teens works, which is different from the way a mom with an empty nest works. We need to think about planning careers that will shift with the seasons of our lives.

Many women in this book are doing just that, sometimes without even realizing it. Suellen Mazurowski is one. This Ohio mom started back for her law degree at age thirty-nine and now runs a small private practice. We met her daughter, Margo Litzenberg, while writing our first book about making the choice to stay home. When we first chatted with Margo several years ago, she was living on a U.S. Navy base in Jacksonville, Florida. Her husband, Shane, a pilot, was on an aircraft carrier in the Persian Gulf, and Margo had left her part-time teaching job to be a full-time, hands-on parent. Shane had a six-year military commitment, and Margo herself had made a similar commitment to her family. "My time will come," she told us.

In 2003, Margo's husband completed his military service and the family moved to Alexandria, Virginia, where he started a new job selling surgical instruments. They are the parents of three-year-old Kerryanne and six-year-old Jacob. With the move, Margo realized that her time had indeed come. She had always planned on law school, following in her mother's footsteps.

However, during her years at home dealing with her son, who was diagnosed with attention deficit/hyperactivity disorder, Margo had made a new discovery about herself. Jacob, born two months prematurely, had undergone dozens of medical tests and visited innumerable doctors in an effort to help him with developmental problems. "We went to so many doctors who wanted to put him on different drugs, and we got all sorts of diagnoses. Because he's small, one doctor wanted to put him on growth hormones, and it was only after I researched it did I find out that there's a possible cancer link and I said no."

When Margo sat down with her husband and mother and talked about her career plans, she realized that her calling was not law but rather child psychology as a result of her experiences as a mom. "I felt backed into a corner by some of these medical decisions. I realized that I could help other parents and children face some of these issues and learn how to deal with them. I feel because of what I have been through, I have a unique perspective and a gift to offer to someone else."

That career path will require a two-year master's program in either social work or child psychology. Margo is conflicted, like many moms facing a change in a life that has settled into a comfortable routine. "I feel frightened and worried about how I am going to be a good wife and mother and also be true to myself and provide myself with intellectual challenges. I feel pressure to go full throttle and jump in with two feet into school. But then my daughter would be in day care and I don't want to do that."

As we chatted, we told Margo what we learned from the many women we interviewed for this book: It does not have to be all or nothing. She can start school part-time and attend classes while her daughter is in nursery school, or at night and weekends when her husband is home. By the time her daughter is in first grade, Margo, armed with her newly minted degree, will be ready to look for a job . . . probably on flextime. So we urged Margo to take that momentous first step and visit the guidance counselor at a local university.

By the end of the conversation, Margo sounded relieved and ready to see if she could start with one course in the fall semester. As she thanked us for our advice, we told her we thank all the women in this book, including her mother, for their pioneering efforts to cut paths where few had ventured before. These women are not rejecting work for motherhood, they are doing something even more daring: They are reinventing work, finding new ways to combine career and family. They don't see a career path as one long hike uphill. Instead the path meanders a bit, taking an occasional detour. They stop to smell the flowers along the way. Sometimes they stroll, other times they racewalk. If the path comes to a dead end, they cut their own trail, starting their own businesses or finding smaller organizations willing to take a chance. These pioneers are a new generation of working women. Others will surely follow.

Notes

Introduction

1. Alfred P. Sloan Center Newsletter, June 2001, www.sloanworkingfamilies.-org/pdfs/newsletter0601pdf.
2. Phyllis Moen, *It's About Time: Couples and Careers* (New York: ILR Press, Cornell University Press, 2003).
3. Pamela Paul, "What Moms Want Now," *Redbook,* March 2003.
4. U.S. Department of Labor, Bureau of Labor Statistics, *BLS Releases 2000–2010 Employment Projections,* www.bls.gov/emp.

One: Making the Decision

1. Mothers and More member survey, 1998, www.mothersandmore.org.
2. Mona Behan and Jeannine Davis-Kimball, Ph.D. *Warrior Women: An Archaeologist's Search for History's Hidden Heroines* (New York: Warner Books, 2003).
3. Carolyn Males, Carol Barbier Rolnick, and Pamela M. Goresh, *Wish You Were Here! A Guide to Baltimore City for Natives and Newcomers* (Maryland: Woodholme House Publishing, 1999).

Two: Getting Going

1. Joan Williams, *Unbending Gender: Why Family and Work Conflict and What to Do About It* (New York: Oxford University Press, 2001).

2. Patricia V. Alea and Patricia Ann Mullins, *The Best Work of Your Life* (New York: Perigee, 1998).

Three: Work That Works

1. *The Practice*, season 7, ABC Television.
2. Sue Shellenbarger, "If You'd Rather Work in Pajamas, Here Are Ways to Talk the Boss into Flex-time," *The Wall Street Journal*, February 13, 2003.
3. Hewitt Associates press release, May 13, 2002. www.hewitt.com/hewitt/-resource/newsroom.
4. Deloitte, *2002 Women's Initiative Annual Report*, www.deloitte.com.
5. American Staffing Association, www.staffingtoday.net/staffstats.
6. AFL-CIO, *Ask a Working Woman Survey 2002*, May 2002, www.aflcio.org.
7. Hewitt Associates May 2002 survey, alternative work arrangements section, *Work/Life Benefits Provided by Major U.S. Employers 2001–2002*.
8. U.S. Department of Labor, Bureau of Labor Statistics, *Workers on Flexible and Shift Schedules in 2001*, www.bls.gov/cps.
9. U.S. Department of Labor, Bureau of Labor Statistics, glossary, www.bls.-gov/bls/glossary.htm.
10. Center for Work and Family Balance. *Fact Sheet 3—Searching for Solutions: Alternative Employment Opportunities*, www.workandfamily.org/research/-factsheets.
11. U.S. Department of Labor, Women's Bureau, *20 Leading Occupations of Employed Women Full-time Wage and Salary Workers 2002 Annual Averages*, www.dol.gov/wb/factsheets.
12. National Teacher Recruitment Clearinghouse, www.recruitingteachers.org.

Four: Starting Your Own Business

1. Center for Women's Business Research, *Women-Owned Businesses in 2002*, www.nfwbo.org/Research/7-16-2002/7-16-2002.htm.
2. Center for Women's Business Research, *Top Ten Facts About Women Business Owners*, www.nfwbo.org/key.html.
3. Center for Women's Business Research, *Seizing the Opportunities: A Report on the Forces Propelling the Growth of Women-Owned Enterprises*, underwritten by Wells Fargo, June 2003.
4. Center for Women's Business Research, *Home-Based Women-Owned Businesses Number and Employ Millions*, www.nfwbo.org/Research/11-16-1995/11-16-1995.htm.

5. Advancing Women Business Center, *SOHO—Small Office, Home Office,* www.advancingwomen.com/soho.html.

6. Business Women's Network WOW Facts 2002, *Home Office and Home Business,* chapter 12, www.ewowfacts.com.

7. Business Women's Network WOW Facts 2003, *Home Office and Home Business,* chapter 23, www.ewowfacts.com.

8. The U.S. Small Business Administration's Online Women's Business Center, *Ten Traits Shared by Winners,* www.onlinewbc.gov.

9. Lisa M. Roberts, *How to Raise a Family and a Career Under One Roof: A Parent's Guide to Home Business* (Texas: Bookhaven, 1997).

10. Paul Edwards, Lisa M. Roberts, and Sarah Edwards, *The Entrepreneurial Parent: How to Earn Your Living and Still Enjoy Your Family, Your Work, and Your Life* (New York: J. P. Tarcher, 2002).

Five: The Family Challenge

1. Laraine T. Zappert, *Getting It Right: How Working Mothers Successfully Take Up the Challenge of Life, Family, and Career* (New York: Simon & Schuster, 2001).

2. Arlie Hochschild, *The Second Shift: Working Parents and the Revolution at Home* (New York: Penguin, 2003).

3. National Partnership for Women and Families, *Balancing Acts: Work/Family Issues on Prime-Time TV,* www.nationalpartnership.org.

4. Michele Kremen Bolton, *The Third Shift: Managing Hard Choices in Our Careers, Homes, and Lives as Women* (New York: Jossey-Bass, 2000).

5. A. Rae Simpson, *Raising Teens: A Synthesis of Research and a Foundation for Action,* Project on the Parenting of Adolescents, Center for Health Communication (Harvard School of Public Health, 2001).

6. Gail Sheehy, *New Passages: Mapping Your Life Across Time* (New York: Ballantine, 1996).

7. Kurt Sandholtz, Brooklyn Derr, Kathy Buckner, and Dawn Carlson, *Beyond Juggling: Rebalancing Your Busy Life* (San Francisco: Berrett-Koehler, 2002).

8. National Partnership for Women & Families, *Family Matters: A National Survey of Women and Men,* 1998, www.nationalpartnership.org.

Six: Workplace Culture Shock

1. Hank Karp, Connie Fuller, and Danilo Sirias, *Bridging the Boomer Xer Gap: Creating Authentic Teams for High Performance at Work* (Palo Alto, CA: Davies-Black Publishing, 2002).

Seven: Getting the Job

1. Wendy S. Enelow and Louise M. Kursmark, *Expert Résumés for People Returning to Work* (Indianapolis: Jist Works, 2003).
2. Caryl Rae Krannich and Ronald L. Krannich, *Nail the Job Interview! 101 Dynamite Answers to Interview Questions* (Manassas Park, VA: Impact Publications, 2003).
3. Douglas Stone, Bruce Patton, and Sheila Heen, *Difficult Conversations: How to Discuss What Matters Most* (New York: Penguin, 2000).

Acknowledgments

While the idea for this book grew out of our own experiences and conversations, it could not have blossomed without the dozens upon dozens of women who told us the tales of their triumphs and their failures as well as the lessons learned along the way. We are grateful to all of them. Some we met personally, others we interviewed on the phone, and still others we corresponded with via e-mail.

While these mothers shared their stories, other people must be credited for helping us turn those tales into a book. Our agent, John Wright, understood our concept immediately. As the father of three daughters—all young mothers with professional careers—he "got it" and sought an editor who embraced our ideas. Jane Rosenman, our first editor at St. Martin's Press, helped us turn the proposal into a book. She passed the baton to Elizabeth Beier, who cheered us to the finish line and beyond. We thank her for her excellent editing and many other right-on-target suggestions.

As we embarked on our research we discovered an academic cornucopia of resources on work/life issues. We want to thank those experts whose research and insights added to our reporting. Providing invaluable assistance at both the early and later stages of the research were Phyllis Moen, who holds the McKnight Presidential Chair in sociology at the University of Minnesota, and Joan Williams, director of Worklife Law at American University's Washington College of Law. An overview of work/life studies was provided by Kathleen Christensen, program director for the Alfred P. Sloan Foundation's Workplace, Workforce and Working Families project, and Robert Drago, professor of labor studies and women's studies, Pennsylvania State University. Shelley MacDermid, director of the Purdue University Center for Families, provided insight on several issues, including part-time work. Of great help on family issues were Linda Waite, codirector of the University of Chicago's Alfred P. Sloan Center on Parents, Children, and Work, and A. Rae Simpson, program director for Parenting Education and Research at the MIT Center for Work, Family, and Personal Life. Myra Hart, of Harvard Business School, shared her insights into the future direction of work. Bruce Tulgan, the founder of RainmakerThinking, Inc., helped with workplace issues.

Our online survey was greatly aided by Mothers and More, especially Pam Hainlin and Debra Levy, who helped with the question design and then by posting a link on their national Web site. And the responses poured in once iVillage linked its Web site to the survey.

We also thank the following women (all moms) for their ideas and input along the way: Bernadette Cain, Annie Gilbar, Sharon

Korman, Silvia Rowney, Vivien Orbach Smith, and Dot Whalen.

The first draft of the completed manuscript greatly benefited from the suggestions and editing of Judy Serrin, and we are most appreciative. The final version was deftly handled by Cynthia Merman. And Lynn Langway was always available as a creative inspiration.

We also want to thank two NYU graduate students, Mackenzie Dawson Parks and Natalie Levine, for their help with transcribing interviews and research. Mackenzie was also our survey stalwart, ably compiling the results as well as giving us an important twentysomething perspective on nine-to-five office life.

Perhaps most important are our families:

Mary: The bulk of the research and writing of this book took place during an incredibly stressful time while my eldest son, Brendan, a marine lieutenant, was deployed to Iraq during the war and its aftermath. I am most thankful to my husband, Frank, for his love and encouragement, especially through that difficult time. He was a sounding board for ideas and offered many suggestions on the various drafts. As my three children, Brendan, Sean, and Colleen, have grown and changed, so has my work life, and through it all they have been a constant source of support and love.

Loretta: As mothers we learn that life's ups and downs cannot be scheduled like after-school activities. While I anguished with Mary and her family during Brendan's deployment, I had the pleasure of planning two weddings for my children, Liz and Jim. The writing and reporting for the book were bracketed by Jim and Julia's wedding in August 2002, and Liz and David's wedding thirteen months later. In fact, my daughter's wedding took place one week after our manuscript was turned over to St. Martin's Press. It still amazes me that the wedding dinner seating plan wasn't mistakenly submitted with the manuscript. Thank you, Liz and Jim, for your patience and support during those very unwieldy days of wedding plans and rewrites. But it is my devoted husband, Vic, who always cheers me on. It is his love, confidence, and support that help me reach new heights. Thank you, Vic.

A final word: In this book we preached what we practice. We like to say that we "job share" being authors, and indeed we do. Through the good times and the difficult times, through the quiet spells and the incredibly busy periods, we have found that being writing partners is the work that works for both of us, and for that we are most grateful.

Index